Contemporary's Whole Language Series

EXPRESSIONS

S T O R I E S   A N D   P O E M S

Contemporary's Whole Language Series

EXPRESSIONS

STORIES AND POEMS

VOLUME 2

Pat Fiene
Project Editor

Ted Knight
Research and Development

CB

CONTEMPORARY BOOKS

a division of NTC/CONTEMPORARY PUBLISHING GROUP
Lincolnwood, Illinois USA

Library of Congress Cataloging-in-Publication Data
(Revised for vol. 2)

Expressions : stories and poems.

(Contemporary's whole language series)
1. Readers (Adult).   2. Readers.   I. Fiene,
Pat.   II. Series.
PE1126.A4E97   1991   428.6   91-25363
ISBN 0-8092-3648-6 (v. 2 : pbk.)

0 1 2 3 4 5 6 7 8 9   QB(M) 15 14 13 12 11 10 9 8 7 6
ISBN: 0-8092-3648-6

Published by Contemporary Books,
a division of NTC/Contemporary Publishing Group, Inc.,
4255 West Touhy Avenue,
Lincolnwood (Chicago), Illinois, 60712-1975 U.S.A.
© 1994 by NTC/Contemporary Publishing Group, Inc.
Manufactured in the United States of America

Editorial Director
Mark Boone

Editorial
Lisa Black
Craig Bolt
Eunice Hoshizaki

Editorial Assistant
Maggie McCann

Editorial Production Manager
Norma Underwood

Cover Design
Georgene Sainati

Cover Illustrator
Kathy Petrauskas

Fine Art Consultant
Steven Diamond

Typography
Terrence Alan Stone

TO THE READER

Welcome to *Expressions*, Volume 2. Take a few minutes to thumb through this book. No matter what kind of story or poem you like, you're bound to find something that interests you.

Do you enjoy funny stories and poems? Read "My Tocaya," Sandra Cisneros's comical tale of a girl who "rises from the dead." Or laugh at Ishmael Reed's comical complaints about women in the poem ".05."

Are mysteries more your style? Try out your detective skills on Henry Slesar's "The Right Kind of House." Try to figure out how a woman will get even with her husband in J. California Cooper's "$100 and Nothing!"

Celebrate the love between parent and child with Amy Tan's "Two Kinds" or W. D. Ehrhart's "Small Song for Daddy." Feel the pain of separation in "Mother" and "Trip in a Summer Dress."

After you read a story or a poem, take time out to reflect and to write. Draw on your own experiences to understand the experiences of the people you read about. On your way to understanding them, you will come to understand more about yourself.

We hope that you enjoy *Expressions*, Volume 2.

The Editors

CONTENTS

Note to the Instructor: The teacher's guide contains a step-by-step lesson plan and activities for every story and poem.

Ishmael Reed is a distinguished and popular African-American writer who has won many awards.

Have you ever been unlucky in love? As you read, imagine how the speaker feels. Does he mean everything he says?

.05

Ishmael Reed

If i had a nickel
For all the women who've
Rejected me in my life
I would be the head of the
World Bank with a flunkie[1]
To hold my derby[2] as i
Prepared to fly chartered[3]
Jet to sign a check
Giving India a new lease
On life

If i had a nickel for
All the women who've loved
Me in my life i would be
The World Bank's assistant
Janitor and wouldn't need
To wear a derby
All i'd think about would
Be going home

---

[1]flunkie: assistant who does unpleasant tasks
[2]derby: stiff, formal hat
[3]chartered: rented

REFLECT ·····································

When you read a poem, do not automatically pause
at the end of each line. Instead, group words
together in meaningful chunks. Pause as you would
in normal conversation. The lines in ".05" could be
arranged to form three sentences. If you were putting
the poem in sentence form, where would you
punctuate with periods? Read the poem out loud,
pausing longer at these points.

How does the speaker feel about his relationships
with women?

Is the speaker serious about what he says, or is he
joking? How can you tell?

What would the speaker do if he had a nickel for
every woman who has ever rejected him? Contrast
these actions with what he would do if he had a
nickel for every woman who has ever loved him.

What does the speaker mean when he says he would
"sign a check / Giving India a new lease / On life"?

WRITE ····································

If the speaker were wealthy, he'd hire an assistant, fly in a private jet, and give a fortune to charity. Explain what you would do if you had millions of dollars.

In your opinion, why have women rejected the speaker so often? Imagine that you are one of the women who rejected him. Write him a letter telling why you don't want to see him again. If you want, use the following beginning to get started.

Dear John,
I'm sorry to say that I'm leaving you because you are just too . . .

Write a poem in the same two-part form as ".05." Begin each part with "If I had a nickel / for every time . . ."

Gerhard Richter, *Kitchen Chair*, 1965, oil on canvas
Collection Kunsthalle Recklinghausen
Courtesy Marian Goodman Gallery

Jerome Weidman has written novels, stories, and plays. His play Fiorello! *won a Pulitzer Prize in 1957.*

How well do you really know the people closest to you? In this story, the speaker's father has a strange habit that puzzles and disturbs his son. As you read, ask yourself why the father sits in the dark.

My Father Sits in the Dark

Jerome Weidman

My father has a peculiar habit. He is fond of sitting in the dark, alone. Sometimes I come home very late. The house is dark. I let myself in quietly because I do not want to disturb my mother. She is a light sleeper. I tiptoe into my room and undress in the dark. I go to the kitchen for a drink of water. My bare feet make no noise. I step into the room and almost trip over my father. He is sitting in a kitchen chair, in his pajamas, smoking his pipe.

"Hello, Pop," I say.

"Hello, son."

"Why don't you go to bed, Pa?"

"I will," he says.

But he remains there. Long after I am asleep I feel sure that he is still sitting there, smoking.

Many times I am reading in my room. I hear my mother get the house ready for the night. I hear my kid brother go to bed. I hear my sister come in. I hear her do things with jars and combs until she, too, is quiet. I know she has gone to sleep. In a little while I hear my mother say good night to my father. I continue to read. Soon I become thirsty. (I drink a lot of water.)

I go to the kitchen for a drink. Again I almost stumble across my father. Many times it startles me. I forget about him. And there he is—smoking, sitting, thinking.

"Why don't you go to bed, Pop?"

"I will, son."

But he doesn't. He just sits there and smokes and thinks. It worries me. I can't understand it. What can he be thinking about? Once I asked him.

"What are you thinking about, Pa?"

"Nothing," he said.

Once I left him there and went to bed. I awoke several hours later. I was thirsty. I went to the kitchen. There he was. His pipe was out. But he sat there, staring into a corner of the kitchen. After a moment I became accustomed to the darkness. I took my drink. He still sat and stared. His eyes did not blink. I thought he was not even aware of me. I was afraid.

"Why don't you go to bed, Pop?"

"I will, son," he said. "Don't wait up for me."

"But," I said, "you've been sitting here for hours. What's wrong? What are you thinking about?"

"Nothing, son," he said. "Nothing. It's just restful. That's all."

The way he said it was convincing. He did not seem worried. His voice was even and pleasant. It always is. But I could not understand it. How could it be restful to sit alone in an uncomfortable chair far into the night, in darkness?

What can it be?

I review all the possibilities. It can't be money. I know that. We haven't much, but when he is worried about money he makes no secret of it. It can't be his health. He is not reticent[1] about that either. It can't be

---

[1]reticent: unwilling to talk

the health of anyone in the family. We are a bit short on money, but we are long on health. (Knock wood, my mother would say.) What can it be? I am afraid I do not know. But that does not stop me from worrying.

Maybe he is thinking of his brothers in the old country. Or of his mother and two step-mothers. Or of his father. But they are all dead. And he would not brood[2] about them like that. I say brood, but it is not really true. He does not brood. He does not even seem to be thinking. He looks too peaceful, too, well not contented, just too peaceful, to be brooding. Perhaps it is as he says. Perhaps it is restful. But it does not seem possible. It worries me.

If I only knew what he thinks about. If I only knew that he thinks at all. I might not be able to help him. He might not even need help. It may be as he says. It may be restful. But at least I would not worry about it.

Why does he just sit there, in the dark? Is his mind failing? No, it can't be. He is only fifty-three. And he is just as keen-witted[3] as ever. In fact, he is the same in every respect. He still likes beet soup. He still reads the second section of the *Times* first. He still wears wing collars.[4] He still believes that Debs[5] could have saved the country and that T.R.[6] was a tool of the moneyed interests. He is the same in every way. He does not even look older than he did five years ago. Everybody remarks about that. Well-preserved, they

---

[2]brood: worry deeply
[3]keen-witted: sharp
[4]wing collars: stiff, early-1900s collars
[5]Debs: Eugene Debs, early-1900s socialist candidate for U.S. president
[6]T.R.: Theodore Roosevelt, U.S. president (1901–1909)

say. But he sits in the dark, alone, smoking, staring straight ahead of him, unblinking, into the small hours of the night.

If it is as he says, if it is restful, I will let it go at that. But suppose it is not. Suppose it is something I cannot fathom.[7] Perhaps he needs help. Why doesn't he speak? Why doesn't he frown or laugh or cry? Why doesn't he do something? Why does he just sit there?

Finally I become angry. Maybe it is just my unsatisfied curiosity. Maybe I *am* a bit worried. Anyway, I become angry.

"Is something wrong, Pop?"

"Nothing, son. Nothing at all."

But this time I am determined not to be put off. I am angry.

"Then why do you sit here all alone, thinking, till late?"

"It's restful, son. I like it."

I am getting nowhere. Tomorrow he will be sitting there again. I will be puzzled. I will be worried. I will not stop now. I am angry.

"Well, what do you *think* about, Pa? Why do you just sit here? What's worrying you? What do you think about?"

"Nothing's worrying me, son. I'm all right. It's just restful. That's all. Go to bed, son."

My anger has left me. But the feeling of worry is still there. I must get an answer. It seems so silly. Why doesn't he tell me? I have a funny feeling that unless I get an answer I will go crazy. I am insistent.

"But what do you *think* about, Pa? What is it?"

"Nothing, son. Just things in general. Nothing special. Just things."

I can get no answer.

---

[7]fathom: understand

It is very late. The street is quiet and the house is dark. I climb the steps softly, skipping the ones that creak. I let myself in with my key and tiptoe into my room. I remove my clothes and remember that I am thirsty. In my bare feet I walk to the kitchen. Before I reach it I know he is there.

I can see the deeper darkness of his hunched shape. He is sitting in the same chair, his elbows on his knees, his cold pipe in his teeth, his unblinking eyes staring straight ahead. He does not seem to know I am there. He did not hear me come in. I stand quietly in the doorway and watch him.

Everything is quiet, but the night is full of little sounds. As I stand there motionless I begin to notice them. The ticking of the alarm clock on the icebox. The low hum of an automobile passing many blocks away. The swish of papers moved along the street by the breeze. A whispering rise and fall of sound, like low breathing. It is strangely pleasant.

The dryness in my throat reminds me. I step briskly into the kitchen.

"Hello, Pop," I say.

"Hello, son," he says. His voice is low and dream-like. He does not change his position nor shift his gaze.

I cannot find the faucet. The dim shadow of light that comes through the window from the street lamp only makes the room seem darker. I reach for the short chain in the center of the room. I snap on the light.

He straightens up with a jerk, as though he has been struck. "What's the matter, Pop?" I ask.

"Nothing," he says sharply. "Only put out the light."

"What's the matter with the light?" I say. "What's wrong?"

"Nothing," he says. "I don't like the light."

I snap the light off. I drink my water slowly. I must take it easy, I say to myself. I must get to the bottom of this.

"Why don't you go to bed? Why do you sit here so late in the dark?"

"It's nice," he says. "I can't get used to lights. We didn't have lights when I was a boy in Europe."

My heart skips a beat and I catch my breath happily. I begin to think I understand. I remember the stories of his boyhood in Austria. I see the wide-beamed *kretchma*,[8] with my grandfather behind the bar. It is late, the customers are gone, and he is dozing. I see the bed of glowing coals, the last of the roaring fire. The room is already dark, and growing darker. I see a small boy, crouched on a pile of twigs at one side of the huge fireplace, his starry gaze fixed on the dull remains of the dead flames. The boy is my father.

I remember the pleasure of those few moments while I stood quietly in the doorway watching him.

"You mean there's nothing wrong? You just sit in the dark because you like it, Pop?" I find it hard to keep my voice from rising in a happy shout.

"Sure," he says. "I can't think with the light on."

I set my glass down and turn to go back to my room. "Good night, Pop," I say.

"Good night," he says.

Then I remember. I turn back. "What do you think about, Pop?" I ask.

His voice seems to come from far away. It is quiet and even again. "Nothing," he says softly. "Nothing special."

---

[8]*kretchma*: tavern

REFLECT ·····························

What questions does the son keep asking his father? Why does he ask them?

Where did the father live as a boy? Where does he live now?

How does the father feel about the past? How can you tell?

How do you think the writer of the story would answer the following question: How well does a person know the people he or she is close to? Explain your answer.

WRITE ······························

Imagine that you are the son in the story, and write a note to the father explaining why you are worried about him.

Have you ever been puzzled by something that someone close to you did? Describe the experience and your reaction to it.

Do you think that the son has a right to know what his father is thinking? Or does the father have a right to keep his thoughts to himself? Explain which view you agree with.

Have you ever had such strong feelings for someone that he or she was all you could think about? That's the way the speaker in this poem feels. As you read, notice how the writer uses exaggeration to make a point.

When I Hear Your Name

Gloria Fuertes

When I hear your name
I feel a little robbed of it;
it seems unbelievable
that half a dozen letters could say so much.

My compulsion[1] is to blast down every wall with
    your name,
I'd paint it on all the houses,
there wouldn't be a well
I hadn't leaned into
to shout your name there,
nor a stone mountain
where I hadn't uttered[2]
those six separate letters
that are echoed back.

My compulsion is
to teach the birds to sing it,
to teach the fish to drink it,
to teach men that there is nothing
like the madness of repeating your name.

My compulsion is to forget altogether
the other 22 letters, all the numbers,
the books I've read, the poems I've written.

---

[1]compulsion: uncontrollable impulse or desire
[2]uttered: said

To say hello with your name.
To beg bread with your name.
'She always says the same thing,' they'd say when
    they saw me,
and I'd be so proud, so happy, so self-contained.

And I'll go to the other world with your name on my
    tongue,
and all their questions I'll answer with your name
—the judges and saints will understand nothing—
God will sentence me to repeating it endlessly and
    forever.

R EFLECT ·

Which statements in the poem are exaggerations?

What does the speaker mean by the statement "When
I hear your name / I feel a little robbed of it"?

W RITE ·

Is there someone you really like or dislike? Write a
poem that explains how you feel. Begin by finishing
this statement: "When I hear your name, I . . ."

Imagine the speaker giving the poem to the person
she has the compulsion for. How do you think the
person would feel after reading it? Happy? Miserable?
Frightened? Some other emotion? Explain.

Describe a positive compulsion that you had for a
person, place, or thing. How long did the compulsion
last? How did you feel when it was over?

Allen Jones, *Shoe*, 1968, lithograph
Courtesy Petersberg Press

Sandra Cisneros is a popular Mexican-American author. She has written two novels and a collection of stories, Woman Hollering Creek, *from which this story was taken.*

Have you ever felt a mysterious connection to another person, even though you did not know the person very well? The thirteen-year-old speaker of this story feels a special connection to a schoolmate who shares her name. As you read the story, ask yourself how you would describe the speaker's attitude toward the "other Patricia."

My Tocaya[1]

Sandra Cisneros

Have you seen this girl? You must've seen her in the papers. Or then again at Father & Son's Taco Palace No. 2 on Nogalitos. Patricia Bernadette Benavídez, my *tocaya*, five feet, 115 pounds, thirteen years old.

Not that we were friends or anything like that. Sure we talked. But that was before she died and came back from the dead. Maybe you read about it or saw her on TV. She was on all the news channels. They interviewed anyone who knew her. Even the p.e. teacher who *had* to say nice things—*She was full of energy, a good kid, sweet.* Sweet as could be, considering she was a freak. Now why didn't anyone ask me?

Patricia Benavídez. The "son" half of Father & Son's Taco Palace No. 2 even before the son quit.

---

[1]tocaya: person with the same name

That's how this Trish inherited the paper hat and white apron after school and every weekend, bored, a little sad, behind the high counters where customers ate standing up like horses.

That wasn't enough to make me feel sorry for her, though, even if her father *was* mean. But who could blame him? A girl who wore rhinestone earrings and glitter high heels to school was destined for trouble that nobody—not God or correctional institutions—could mend.

I think she got double promoted[2] somewhere and that's how come she wound up in high school before she had any business being here. Yeah, kids like that always try too hard to fit in. Take this *tocaya*—same name as me, right? But does she call herself *la* Patee, or Patty, or something normal? No, she's gotta be different. Says her name's "Tri-ish." Invented herself a phony English accent too, all breathless and sexy like a British Marilyn Monroe. Real goofy. I mean, whoever heard of a Mexican with a British accent? Know what I mean? The girl had problems.

But if you caught her alone, and said, *Pa-trrri-see-ah*—I always made sure I said it in Spanish—*Pa-trrri-see-ah, cut the bull crap and be for real.* If you caught her without an audience, I guess she was all right.

That's how I managed to put up with her when I knew her, just before she ran away. Disappeared from a life sentence at that taco house. Got tired of coming home stinking of crispy tacos. Well, no wonder she left. I wouldn't want to stink of crispy tacos neither.

Who knows what she had to put up with. Maybe her father beat her. He beats her brother, I know that. Or at least they beat each other. It was one of those

---

[2]double promoted: skipped a grade in school

fist fights that finally did it—drove the boy off forever, though probably he was sick of stinking of tacos too. That's what I'm thinking.

Then a few weeks after the brother was gone, this *tocaya* of mine had her picture in all the papers, just like the kids on milk cartons:

HAVE YOU SEEN THIS GIRL?
Patricia Bernadette Benavídez, 13, has been missing since Tuesday, Nov. 11, and her family is extremely worried. The girl, who is a student at Our Lady of Sorrows High School, is believed to be a runaway and was last seen on her way to school in the vicinity of Dolorosa and Soledad. Patricia is 5′, 115 lbs., and was wearing a jean jacket, blue plaid uniform skirt, white blouse, and high heels [*glitter probably*] when she disappeared. Her mother, Delfina Benavídez, has this message: "Honey, call Mommy y te quiero mucho."[3]

Some people.

What did I care Benavídez disappeared? Wouldn't've. If it wasn't for Max Lucas Luna Luna, senior, Holy Cross, our brother school. They sometimes did exchanges with us. Teasers is what they were. Sex Rap Crap is what we called it, only the sisters called them different—Youth Exchanges. Like where they'd invite some of the guys from Holy Cross over here for Theology, and some of us girls from Sorrows would go over there. And we'd pretend like we were real interested in the issue "The Blessed Virgin: Role Model for Today's Young Woman," "Petting: Too Far, Too Fast, Too Late," "Heavy Metal and the Devil." Shit like that.

---

[3]y te quiero mucho: and I love you very much

Not every day. Just once in a while as kind of an experiment. Catholic school was afraid of putting us all together too much, on account of hormones. That's what Sister Virginella said. If you can't conduct yourselves like proper young ladies when our guests arrive, we'll have to suspend our Youth Exchanges indefinitely. No whistling, grabbing, or stomping in the future, *is that clear*?!!!

Alls I know is he's got these little hips like the same size since he was twelve probably. Little waist and little ass wrapped up neat and sweet like a Hershey bar. Damn! That's what I remember.

Turns out Max Lucas Luna Luna lives next door to the freak. I mean, I never even bothered talking to Patricia Benavídez before, even though we were in the same section of General Business. But she comes up to me one day in the cafeteria when I'm waiting for my french fries and goes:

"Hey, *tocaya*, I know someone who's got the hots for[4] you."

"Yeah, right," I says, trying to blow her off. I don't want to be seen talking to no flake.

"You know a guy named Luna from Holy Cross, the one who came over for that Theology exchange, the cute one with the ponytail?"

"So's?"

"Well, he and my brother Ralphie are tight, and he told Ralphie not to tell nobody but he thinks Patricia Chávez is real fine."

"You lie, girl."

"Swear to God. If you don't believe me, call my brother Ralphie."

Shit! That was enough to make me Trish Benavídez's best girlfriend for life, I swear. After that, I

---

[4]got the hots for: attracted to

always made sure I got to General Business class early. Usually she'd have something to tell me, and if she didn't, I made sure to give her something to pass on to Max Lucas Luna Luna. But it was painful slow on account of this girl worked so much and didn't have no social life to speak of.

That's how this Patricia Bernadette got to be our messenger of luh-uv[5] for a while, even though me and Max Lucas Luna Luna hadn't gotten beyond the I-like-you/Do-you-like-me stage. Hadn't so much as seen each other since the rap crap, but I was working on it.

I knew they lived somewhere in the Monte Vista area. So I'd ride my bike up and down streets—Magnolia, Mulberry, Huisache, Mistletoe—wondering if I was hot or cold. Just knowing Max Lucas Luna Luna might appear was enough to make my blood laugh.

The week I start dropping in at Father & Son's Taco Palace No. 2, is when she decides to skip. First we get an announcement over the intercom from Sister Virginella. *I am sorry to have to announce one of our youngest and dearest students has strayed from home. Let us keep her in our hearts and in our prayers until her safe return.* That's when she first got her picture in the paper with her ma's weepy message.

Personally it was no grief or relief to me she escaped so clean. That's for sure. But as it happened, she owed me. Bad enough she skips and has the whole school talking. At least *then* I had hope she'd make good on her promise to hook me up with Max Lucas Luna Luna. But just when I could say her name again without spitting, she goes and dies. Some kids playing in a drain ditch find a body, and yeah, it's her. When the TV cameras arrive at our school, there go all them drama hot shits howling real tears, even the ones that didn't know her. Sick.

---

[5]luh-uv: love

Well, I couldn't help but feel bad for the dip once she's dead, right? I mean, after I got over being mad. Until she rose from the dead three days later.

After they've featured her ma crying into a wrinkled handkerchief and her dad saying, "She was my little princess," and the student body using money from our Padre Island field-trip fund to buy a bouquet of white gladiolus with a banner that reads VIRGENCITA, CUÍDALA,[6] and the whole damn school having to go to a high mass in her honor, my *tocaya* outdoes herself. Shows up at the downtown police station and says, I ain't dead.

Can you believe it? Her parents had identified the body in the morgue and everything. "I guess we were too upset to examine the body properly." Ha!

I never did get to meet Max Lucas Luna Luna, and who cares, right? All I'm saying is she couldn't even die right. But whose famous face is on the front page of the *San Antonio Light*, the *San Antonio Express News, and* the *Southside Reporter*? Girl, I'm telling you.

---

[6]Virgencita, cuídala: Virgin Mother, help her

REFLECT ·

Where does the story take place? What details describe the neighborhood?

Though the speaker doesn't say much about herself directly, her actions and attitude toward her *tocaya* tell a lot about her. What is the speaker like?

Why does the speaker call Patricia a "freak"?

The writer of the story has the speaker use "incorrect" grammar and swearwords. Why? How would it change the story if the speaker spoke "properly"? In your opinion, would it make the story better?

The speaker never has a chance to speak to Max, the teenager she has a crush on. Do you think Patricia told the truth about Max's interest in the speaker? Why or why not?

WRITE ·

Why did Patricia Benavídez leave home? Imagine that you are she, and write a letter explaining why you are leaving.

Where do you think Patricia Benavídez was while everyone was looking for her? Use your imagination to describe the time she spent away from home. Explain why she came back.

Patricia Benavídez's "return from the dead" would be front-page news. Write a short news story giving the facts about her return. Give your story an attention-grabbing headline.

Do fathers feel different toward their daughters than toward their sons? As you read, think about the father's emotions.

Small Song for Daddy

W. D. Ehrhart

It isn't like my daughter
to awake at one a.m.—
but here she is.

She pulls the hairs on my chest
idly,[1] wiggles her toes, sighs
almost as if in meditation,
and begins to sing softly,

the language hers alone,
the voice clear and fragile[2]
as water striking stone.

New in a world where new
is all she knows, she sings
for each new wonder
she discovers—as if those

curtains, the chair, that
box of Kleenex were created
solely to delight her.

And they do. And she sings,
not knowing she is singing
for a father much in need
of her particular song.

---

[1]idly: without purpose
[2]fragile: delicate

REFLECT··································

The poem is about a daughter. How old do you think she is? What details give you clues about her age?

Is the daughter upset, or is she contented? What details tell you so?

What do you think the daughter's song sounds like?

At the end of the poem, why does the father call the baby's song "her particular song"? Why do you think he might be so much in need of his daughter's song?

What do you imagine happened after the events in the poem? Did the daughter go quickly back to sleep? How did the father feel after her song ended?

WRITE ·································

The father in the poem focuses on describing his daughter's voice. Describe someone you admire or love. In your description, focus on one characteristic also, such as voice, eyes, or gestures.

The father says he is "much in need" of his daughter's song. What happened during the day to make him need her song that night? Use your imagination, and describe the father's day.

What do you think the father is feeling most strongly in this poem? Describe a situation in which you felt the same emotion.

Jack Beal, *The Dark Pool*, 1980, pastel on grey paper
Frumkin/Adams Gallery, New York
Photograph: eeva-inkeri

*Have you ever been in a dangerous situ-
ation—perhaps even a life-threatening
one? What thoughts raced through your
mind? Did you concentrate on what was
happening, or did you find yourself
thinking about loved ones and friends?
As you read the story, notice what the
man thinks about as he faces a life-or-
death situation.*

Crossing Spider Creek

Dan O'Brien

Here is a seriously injured man on a frightened horse.
They are high in the Rocky Mountains at the junction
of the Roosevelt Trail and Spider Creek. Tom has tried
to coax[1] the horse into the freezing water twice before.
Both times the horse started to cross then lost its
nerve, swung around violently, and lunged back up the
bank. The pivot[2] and surge[3] of power had been nearly
too much for Tom. Both times he almost lost his grip
on the saddlehorn and fell into the boulders of the
creek bank. Both times, when it seemed his hold
would fail, he had thought of his wife, Carol. He will
try the crossing once more. It will take all the strength
he has left.

This is not the Old West. It is nineteen eighty-
seven, autumn, a nice day near the beginning of elk
season. Two days ago Tom had led the horse, his camp
packed in panniers[4] hung over the saddle, up this

---

[1]coax: persuade
[2]pivot: spin
[3]surge: strong rise
[4]panniers: pair of saddle bags

same trail. He had some trouble getting the horse to cross the creek but it hadn't been bad. This was a colt, Carol's colt and well broke to lead. It had come across without much fuss. But that was before the nice weather had swelled Spider Creek with runoff, and of course the colt had not had the smell of blood in his nostrils.

Tom's injury is a compound fracture of the right femur.[5] He has wrapped it tightly with an extra cotton shirt but he cannot stop the bleeding. The blood covers the right shoulder of the horse, the rifle scabbard,[6] and the saddle from the seat to the stirrup. Tom knows that it is the loss of blood that is making him so weak. He wonders if that is why his thoughts keep wandering from what he is trying to do here, with the horse, to Carol. She has never understood his desire to be alone. From time to time, over the years, she has complained that he cares less for her than for solitude.[7] He has always known that is not true. But still it seems vaguely funny to him that now she is all he wants to think about. He wishes she could know that, hopes he will have a chance to tell her.

Perhaps it is being on this particular horse, he thinks, the one Carol likes better than any of the others. Maybe Carol has spent enough time with this horse to have become part of it.

The horse moves nervously under him as he reins it around to face the water again. Tom wishes there were a way to ease the animal through this. But there is not, and there is clearly little time. There is just this one last chance.

They begin to move slowly down the bank again. It will be all or nothing. If the horse makes it across

---

[5]femur: upper leg bone
[6]scabbard: holder
[7]solitude: being alone

Spider Creek they will simply ride down the trail, be at a campground in twenty minutes. There are other hunters there. They will get him to a hospital. If the horse refuses and spins in fear, Tom will fall. The horse will clamber[8] up the bank and stand aloof, quaking with terror and forever out of reach. Tom sees himself bleeding to death, alone, by the cascading[9] icy water.

As the horse stretches out its nose to sniff at the water, Tom thinks that there might be time, if he falls, to grab at the rifle and drag it from the scabbard as he goes down. He clucks[10] to the horse and it moves forward. Though he would hate to, it might be possible to shoot the horse from where he would fall. With luck he would have the strength to crawl to it and hold its warm head for a few moments before they died. It would be best for Carol if they were found like that.

Here is a seriously injured man on a frightened horse. They are standing at the edge of Spider Creek, the horse's trembling front feet in the water and the man's spurs held an inch from the horse's flanks.[11]

---

[8]clamber: climb with difficulty
[9]cascading: rushing
[10]clucks: makes encouraging sounds
[11]flanks: rear quarters

REFLECT ·····································

Why is it important for Tom to cross Spider Creek? What will happen to him if he is unable to?

Why is Tom having difficulty making his horse cross the creek?

Why is Tom alone in the mountains?

Tom thinks about trying to shoot the horse if he falls off. He believes it would be best for Carol, his wife, if he and the horse were found dead together. Why does he think so?

In your opinion, how does Tom's ordeal end? Does he make it across the creek, or doesn't he? Give reasons for your answer.

WRITE ·····································

Imagine that you are Tom, and write a note to Carol to be found if you don't make it across the creek. Tell her what you were thinking after you failed to cross the creek for the second time.

How do you think Carol feels when Tom prepares for a trip into the mountains? Write a dialogue between Carol and Tom in which she expresses her emotions.

Write a new conclusion for the story. Tell what happened when Tom attempted to cross the creek for the third and last time. Try to make your writing sound like the story writer's.

Has someone's death ever given you the feeling that things were left unsaid or not done? In this poem, a mother dies before her daughter, who lives far away, can see her one more time. As you read, think about the speaker's feelings toward her mother and her death.

Mother

Bea Exner Liu

I wish that I could talk with her again.
That's what I thought of when I thought of home,
Always supposing I had a home to come to.
If she were here, we'd warm the Chinese pot[1]
To brew a jasmine[2]-scented elixir,[3]
And I would tell her how my life has been—
All the parts that don't make sense to me—
And she would let me talk until the parts
Fitted together.

That will never be.
She couldn't wait for me to come to her—
Ten years away. I couldn't wish for her
To wait, all blind and helpless as she was.
So now I have come home to emptiness:

---

[1]pot: teapot
[2]jasmine: flower used as a tea
[3]elixir: drink that restores or preserves health

No silly welcome-rhyme, no happy tears,
No eager questioning. No way to get
An answer to my questions. Silence fills
The rooms that once were cheery with her song,
And all the things I wanted to talk out
With her are locked forever in my heart.

I wander through the rooms where she is not.
Alone I sit on the hassock[4] by her chair,
And there, at last, I seem to hear her voice:
"You're a big girl now. You can work things out."

REFLECT ·····································

What does the daughter think about as she walks
through her mother's house?

What does the daughter miss most about her mother?

Why does the daughter sit next to her mother's
empty chair?

The daughter says nothing about her father. In your
experience, are daughters usually closer to their
mothers or to their fathers? Why?

---

[4]hassock: cushion

WRITE ·····································

The daughter looked forward to her mother's "silly welcome-rhyme," "happy tears," and "eager questioning." List several small things that you look forward to whenever you enter some special or familiar place—your home, a friend's house, a favorite store or restaurant, a co-worker's office. Try to include sights, smells, and sounds.

Write a conversation between the daughter and her mother. Imagine that they are discussing the daughter's life and one of the "parts that don't make sense." What problem might the daughter wish to discuss? What advice would the mother give?

In the last two lines, the daughter imagines her mother talking to her. Does the daughter feel comforted by these imagined words, or do they upset her? Why do you think she feels this way?

Billy Morrow Jackson, *Station*, 1980–82 version, oil on masonite
Courtesy Jane Haslem Gallery, Washington, D.C.

Have you ever had trouble making an important decision? The young woman in the following story has to make a difficult choice. As you read, think about how she feels. In your opinion, does she make the right choice?

Trip in a Summer Dress

Annette Sanford

Moths are already dying under the street lamps when I board the bus. I have said goodbye to my mother and to Matthew, who is crying because he's almost six and knows I won't be back in time for his birthday. I won't be back for the next one either, but who's going to tell him that?

I spread myself out on two seats. I have a brown plastic purse, a tan makeup case, and a paperback book. I could be anybody starting a trip.

The driver is putting the rest of my things in the luggage compartment. His name is E. E. Davis, and the sign at the front of the bus says not to talk to him. He can count on me.

The bus is coughing gray smoke into the loading lanes. I can see my mother and Matthew moving back into the station, out of sight. I fan myself with the paperback and smooth the skirt of my dress. Blue. Cotton. No sleeves.

"It's too late for a summer dress," my mother said while we waited. Before that, she said October is a cold month in Arkansas. She said that Matthew needs vitamins, that the man who sells tickets looks like Uncle Harry. Some things she said twice without even noticing.

We're moving finally.

E. E. Davis is making announcements in a voice like a spoon scraping a cooking pot. *We rest twenty minutes in Huntsville, we stay in our seats while the coach is in motion.* All the time he's talking I'm watching my mother and Matthew on the corner waiting for the light to change. Matthew is sucking two fingers and searching the bus windows for me. I could wave, but I don't.

I'm riding off into the night because two days from now in Eureka Springs, Arkansas, I'm going to be married. Bill Richards is his name. He has brown hair and a gentle touch and a barber shop. He thinks marriages are made in heaven. He thinks Matthew is my mother's son.

She's young enough. She married and had her first child when she was fifteen. So did I, but I wasn't married.

Matthew was born on Uncle Harry's tree farm in East Texas where I went with my mother after she told all her friends she was pregnant again. She needed fresh air and a brother's sympathy, she said, and me to look after her.

Knowing me, maybe some of them believed her.

I was skinny and flat-chested and worked after school in the aviary[1] at the zoo mixing up peanut butter and sunflower seeds and feeding fuzzy orphans with an eye dropper. Most nights I studied. What happened was just a mistake I made because I'd never given much thought to that kind of thing and when the time came it caught me without my mind made up one way or the other.

So we went to the tree farm.

Every day while we waited my mother preached me a sermon: you didn't pass around a child like a

---

[1]aviary: building where birds are kept

piece of cake, and you didn't own him like a house or a refrigerator, and you didn't tell him one thing was true one day and something else was true the next. You took a child and set him down in the safest place you could find. Then you taught him the rules and let him grow. One thing for sure: you didn't come along later just when he was thinking he was a rose and tell him he was a lily instead, just because it suited you to.

What you did was you gave him to your mother and father and you called him your brother and that was that.

Except for one thing. They let you name him.

I picked Matthew because of the dream.

All through that night I'd been Moses' sister tending to the reed basket when the queen found him. All night I was Moses' sister running up and down that river bank hollering till my throat about burst. When the pain was over, there he was—with my mother taking care of him just like the Bible story says. Only you can't name a little pink baby Moses because Moses was mostly an old man. So I settled on Matthew.

It made him mine.

There are four people on this bus. There's a black boy in the second seat blowing bubbles with his gum. Across from him are a couple of ladies just out of the beauty parlor with hair too blue, and a child one seat up across from me. A little girl. Scared probably. She's pretty young for traveling in the dark.

I'm not going to look at them anymore. Everything you do in this life gets mixed up with something else, so you better watch out, even just looking at people. Landscapes are safer.

Pine trees, rice fields, oil rigs. I got my fill of them coming back from Uncle Harry's. I didn't look once at Matthew, but I felt him, even when he wasn't crying. He had hold of me way down deep and wouldn't let go for love nor money.

I sat on the back seat. My father drove and my mother cooed at her brand new son, the first one in four girls. If she said that one time, she said it a hundred.

Finally *I* said—so loud my father ran off the road, "He's not your child! I birthed him. I'm his mother, and I'm going to raise him up to know I am! Now what's the matter with that?"

My mother said, "Count the *I*'s, and you'll know." She didn't even turn around.

I got used to it, the way you do a thorn that won't come out or chronic appendicitis.[2] But it's hard to pretend all the time that something's true when it isn't.

So I didn't.

I talked to Matthew about it. I fed him cereal on the back porch by the banana tree, and I told him just how it was he came about. I took him to the park in his red-striped stroller and showed him pansies and tulips and iris blooming. I told him they were beautiful and that's the way it is with love.

Only I hadn't loved his father, I said, and that's where I was wrong. A person ought never to give his body if his soul can't come along.

I told him I'd never leave him because he was me and I was him, and no matter what his mother—who was really his grandmother—said, I had a plan that would save us.

Then he learned to talk, and I had to quit all that.

It's just as well 'cause look at me now. Leaving. Going away from him as hard and fast as ever I can. Me and E. E. Davis burning up the pavement to Huntsville so we can rest twenty minutes and start up again.

Now here's a town.

---

[2]chronic appendicitis: recurring inflammation of the appendix

That little girl across the aisle is rising up and
squirming around. Maybe she lives here. Maybe one of
those houses going by with lights on and people eating supper inside is hers. But I'm not going to ask. You
get a child started talking, you can't stop them sometimes.

Like Matthew.

The day I said yes to Bill Richards I set my plan a-
going. I took Matthew to the park like I always had. We
sat under a tree where I knew something was likely to
happen because lately it always did, and when it
started, I said: "Looka there, Matthew. See that redbird
feeding her baby?"

"That's not her baby," he said when he finally
found the limb. "She's littler than it."

"That's right. The baby's a cowbird, but it *thinks*
it's a redbird."

He was real interested. "Does the redbird know
it's not her baby?"

"Yes, but she keeps on taking care of it because it
hatched in her nest and she loves it."

"How did it get in her nest?"

"Its mama left it there." I'm taking it slow by
then, being mighty careful. "She gave it to the red-
birds, but just for a little while."

Matthew looked at me. "Mamas don't do that."

"Sometimes they do. If they have to."

"Why would they have to?"

"If they can't take care of the babies, it's better
that way."

"Why can't they take care of them?"

"Well. For one thing, cowbirds are too lazy to
build nests. Or won't. Or can't." I saw right away I'd
said it all wrong.

Matthew stuck out his bottom lip. "I don't like
cowbirds."

"They aren't really bad birds," I said quick as I

could. "They just got started on the wrong foot—
wing." Nothing went right with that conversation.

"They're ugly too."

"The mama comes back, Matthew. She always
comes back. She whistles and the baby hears and they
fly away together."

"I wouldn't go. I'd peck her with my nose."

"Let's go look at the swans," I said.

"I'd tell her to go away and never come back."

"Maybe you'd like some popcorn."

"I would be a redbird forever!"

"Or peanuts. How about a nice big bag?"

When we got home he crawled up in my mother's
lap and kissed her a million times. He told her cowbirds are awful. He told her he was mighty glad he
belonged to her and not to a cowbird. She was mighty
glad too, she said.

I told her now was the time to set things straight
and she could be a plenty big help if she wanted to.

She told me little pitchers have big ears.[3]

Eureka Springs is about the size of this town we're
going through. In Eureka Springs the barber shop of
Bill Richards is set on a mountain corner, he says, and
the streets drop off like shelves around it. Eureka
Springs is a tourist place. Christ[4] stands on a hill there
and sees the goings-on. In Eureka Springs, Bill Richards has a house with window boxes in the front and
geraniums growing out, just waiting for someone to
pick them.

I can see people in these houses in this town
hanging up coats and opening doors and kissing each
other. Women are washing dishes, and kids are getting
lessons.

---

[3]little pitchers have big ears: children overhear things they
shouldn't
[4]Christ: statue of Christ

Next year Matthew is going to school in Houston.
My mother will walk with him to the corner where
he'll catch the bus. He'll have on short pants and a red
shirt because red's his favorite color, and he won't
want to let go of her hand. In Eureka Springs it will be
too cool for a boy to start school wearing short pants.

In Eureka Springs, a boy won't have to.

I can see I was wrong about that little girl. She's
not scared. She's been up and down the aisle twice
and pestered E. E. Davis. She's gotten chewing gum
from the boy and candy from the ladies. It's my turn
now, I guess.

"Hello." I know better, but I can't help it.

She puts a sticky hand on my arm. "How come
you're crying?"

"Dirt in my eye."

"From the chemical plant," she says, pretty
smarty. "They're p'luters.[5] They make plastic bags and
umber-ellas."

I open my purse and take out a Kleenex. "How do
you know?"

"I know everything on this road."

"You live on it?"

She throws back her head like a TV star. "Prac'ly.[6]
Fridays I go that way." She points toward the back
window. "Sundays I come back. My daddy's got week-
in custardy."[7]

She hangs on the seat in front of me and breathes
through her mouth. She smells like corn chips. "They
had a big fight, but Mama won most of me. You got any
kids?"

"No—yes."

---

[5]p'luters: polluters
[6]prac'ly: practically
[7]week-in custardy: weekend custody; the child lives with
her father on the weekends

"Don't you know?" A tooth is missing under those pouty lips.

"I have a boy, a little younger than you." I never said it out loud before to anybody but Matthew, and him when he was just a baby.

"Where is he?"

"At home. With his grandmother."

"Whyn't you bring him?"

"I'm going a far piece. He's better off there."

She pops her gum and swings a couple of times on one heel. "You got a boyfriend?"

"Yes." It's out before I can stop it. I ought to bite my tongue off or shake her good. A child with no manners is an abomination[8] before the Lord, my mother says. That's one thing about my mother. She won't let Matthew get away with a thing.

The child turns up her mouth corners, but it's not a smile. "My mama's got one too. Name's Rex. He's got three gold teeth and a Cadillac."

"How far is it to Huntsville?"

"Two more towns and a dance hall."

"You run on. I'm going to take a nap."

She wanders off up the aisle and plops in a seat. In a second her feet are up in it, her skirt sky-high. Somebody ought to care that she does that. Somebody ought to be here to tell her to sit up like a lady. Especially on a bus. All kinds of people ride buses.

I met Bill Richards on a bus. Going to Galveston for Splash Day. He helped us off and carried my tote bag and bought us hot dogs. He bought Matthew a snow cone. He built him a castle. He gave him a shoulder ride right into the waves. A girl married to Bill Richards wouldn't have to do a thing but love him.

---

[8]abomination: hateful thing

A girl married to Bill Richards wouldn't tell him she had a son with no father, my mother said. And she wouldn't tell her son he was her son. Or a redbird either. She would forget it and love her brother.

We're stopping at a filling station sort of place. The blue-haired ladies are tying nets around their heads and stuffing things in paper sacks. They get out and a lot of hot air comes in. The door pops shut and E. E. Davis gives it the gas. "Ten more miles to Huntsville."

"My mama better be there this time!" the child says, loud and quivery. I had it right in the first place, I guess. Her scare is just all slicked over with chewing gum and smart talk. Inside she's powerful shaky.

"Your mama'll be there, don't you worry." Before I can close my mouth she's on me like a plaster cast. I should have been a missionary.

"She's always late. Last time I waited all night. The bus station man bought me a cheese sandwich and covered me up with his coat."

"Something kept her, I guess."

"Yeah." She slides down in the seat beside me. "Rex."

I don't want to talk to her. I want to think about things. I want to figure out how it's going to be in Eureka Springs with Christ looking right into the kitchen window when I'm kissing Bill Richards, and Him knowing all the time about Moses' sister. I want to think about Matthew growing up and getting married himself and even dying without ever knowing I'm his mother.

Most of all I want to get off this bus and go and get my baby.

"Huntsville!" yells E. E.

"I told you! I told you she wouldn't be here." That child's got a grip on my left hand so tight the blood's quit running. We're standing in the waiting room with lots of faces, but none of them is the right one. It's pitch dark outside and hot as a devil's poker.

"Just sit down," I say. "She'll come."

"I have to go to the bathroom."

"Go ahead. I'll watch for her."

I go in the phone booth. No matter what my mother says, Matthew is a big boy. He can take it. So can Bill Richards. I put two quarters and seven nickels on the shelf by the receiver. I get the dial tone. I spin the numbers out, eleven of them, and drop my money in the slot.

I see the woman coming in out of the dark. She's holding hands with a gold-toothed man and her mouth's all pouty like the child's. My mother's voice shouts hello in my ear.

"Wait," I tell her.

I open the door of the phone booth. "Wait! She's in the restroom. Your child. There, she's coming yonder."

I can see they wish she wasn't. I can see how they hate Sundays.

"Talk if you're going to," my mother says. She only calls long distance when somebody dies.

"Mama, I wanted to tell you—"

"That you wish you had your coat. I knew it! The air's too still and sticky not to be breeding a blizzard."[9]

"It's *hot* here, for goodness sakes!"

"Won't be for long. Thirty by morning the TV says. Twenty where you're going. Look in the makeup case. I stuck in your blue wool sweater."

"Matthew—"

---

[9]breeding a blizzard: producing a storm

"In bed and finally dropping off. I told him an hour ago, the sooner you shed today, the quicker to-morrow'll come,[10] but he's something else to convince, that boy."

"Comes by it naturally," I say, and plenty loud, but she doesn't hear.

"Have a good trip," she's yelling, "and wrap up warm in the wind."

When I step outside, it's blowing all right, just like she said. Hard from the north and sharp as a scissors.

By the time E. E. Davis swings open the door and bellows, "All aboard for Eureka Springs," that wind is tossing up newspapers and bus drivers' caps and hems of summer dresses. It's whipping through door cracks and rippling puddles and freezing my arms where the sleeves ought to be.

If I was my mother, I'd get mighty tired of always being right.

REFLECT ·

Where is the young woman in the story going? Why is she going there?

The young woman says, "The day I said yes to [agreed to marry] Bill Richards I set my plan a-going." What was her plan? Why didn't she stick to it?

---

[10]the sooner you shed today, the quicker tomorrow'll come: the sooner you go to sleep, the quicker it will be tomorrow

Why does the young woman call Matthew's attention to the birds in the park? What do the mother and baby cowbird represent?

What does the young woman plan to do when she goes into the telephone booth in Huntsville? What does she actually do? Why do you think she changed her mind?

In your opinion, has the young woman chosen the right future for herself? For her son?

WRITE ···································

In your opinion, who was right—the young woman or her mother? Make a list of reasons why you agree with the person. Organize the list so that it begins with the weakest, or least convincing, reason and ends with the strongest, or most convincing, reason.

Like the young woman in the story, we all have to make difficult decisions from time to time. Write about a hard choice you once had to make. Explain how you felt and whether you were happy with your decision.

Imagine that you are the young woman. Write a page in your diary explaining how you feel as the bus nears Bill Richards and your new home in Eureka Springs.

Have you ever treasured an object be-
cause it reminds you of a loved one who's
now gone? The speaker in the poem
below describes some small things that his
father left behind. As you read, think
about the father's influence on his son.

Leaves

H. S. Hamod

for my children, David and Laura

Tonight, Sally and I are making stuffed
grapeleaves,[1] we get out a package, it's
drying out, I've been saving it in the freezer, it's
one of the last things my father ever picked in this
life—they're over five years old
and up to now
we just kept finding packages of them in the
freezer, as if he were still picking them
somewhere   packing them
carefully to send to us
making sure they didn't break into pieces.

* * *

"To my Dar Garnchildn
Davd and Lura
from Thr Jido"
twisted on tablet paper
between the lines
in this English lettering

---

[1]stuffed grapeleaves: dish made by wrapping grape leaves
around a meat filling

hard for him even to print,
I keep this small torn record,
this piece of paper stays in the upstairs storage,
one of the few pieces of American
my father ever wrote.   We find his Arabic letters
all over the place, even in the files we find
letters to him in English, one I found from Charles
    Atlas[2]
telling him, in 1932,
"Of course, Mr. Hamod, you too can build
your muscles like mine . . ."

* * *

Last week my mother told me, when I was
asking why I became a poet, "But don't you
    remember,
your father made up poems, don't you remember
    him
singing in the car as we drove—those were poems."
Even now, at night, I sometimes
get out the Arabic grammar book
though it seems so late.

---

[2]Charles Atlas: famous bodybuilder whose courses were
advertised in many popular magazines

Reflect ·····································

How long has the speaker's father been dead? What was the father's native language?

What things has the speaker saved as reminders of his father?

The father had difficulty writing in English. What message did he write on the piece of tablet paper? What does the message tell you about him?

What influence has the father had on the speaker?

Write ··································

The speaker got a love of poetry from his father. What likes (or dislikes) have your parents or other family members passed on to you? Describe a few.

What objects do you keep in memory of a loved one? Describe one, telling who the object reminds you of and how it makes you feel.

The speaker has saved a short written message for his children to remember their grandfather by. What message would you like to leave behind? Think of someone you are close to. Write the person a letter to be opened after your death.

Carol Poticny, *Barber Shop*, 1990, etching

Charles Baxter's stories are regularly chosen to appear in Best American Short Stories. *He has won many awards for his writing, which includes short stories, poems, and novels.*

How does it feel to talk to someone you used to love and haven't seen in a long time? The woman and man in the story below have very different emotions. As you read, look for clues that tell you about their earlier relationship.

Scissors

Charles Baxter

The barber, whose name was Harold, had read the sports section, the business news, and was working his way down the front page when the boy and his mother came inside. The boy was wearing a spring coat too large for him, with mittens attached to the coat sleeves with alligator clips. The woman, upon entering, stood up straight as the barber looked at her and dropped his paper onto the floor.

"Louise," he said, and the woman nodded. It was midday, and there were no other customers and no other barbers. Outside, the ice had melted into puddles, and the boy was stamping his feet. The woman and the barber stood looking at each other until finally he said, "Louise, it's been a coon's age."[1]

"Has it been that long?" she asked. She dropped her spring coat on one of the chairs, helped her son out of his hat and coat, and led him toward the first

---

[1]coon's age: very long time

barber chair. "Such a nice day," she said. "Like spring, even though it *isn't* spring yet. Time for Robbie's first professional haircut. And I thought, well, certainly, you should do it." She leaned forward and kissed the barber on the cheek.

"I've seen you around town," he said. "Sometimes I wave, but you never seem to see me."

She smiled. "Oh," she said, "I see you. And I always think, 'Well, there's Harold, and he's waving at me,' and what I do is, I sort of wave back, but, you know, mentally. Not so anyone would see."

They stood there for a moment, the barber looking at the woman's face, doing his best not to stare at it, and the woman turned in profile to him, gazing at the display of Pinaud Clubman aftershave and Lucky Tiger hair tonic on the windowsill. Her hands were on her son's shoulders.

"Did you know, Harold, that they're going to send a hot air balloon down, well, I mean, just *over* the main street in a little while? I heard about it."

"It's a promotion,"[2] he said. "Tulip Days in Five Oaks.[3] They're going to drop discount coupons from the balloon into the street. It's good for business." He was tugging nervously at his mustache. He stopped himself and went over to the counter near the mirror and came back with a board, which he put over the arms of the chair. He hoisted[4] the boy up on the board and tucked the cloth in around his neck and spread it over his shirt and pants. The boy squirmed for a moment.

The barber bent down. "So, how old are you, young man?"

---

[2]promotion: attention-grabbing sales event
[3]Five Oaks: town in which the story takes place
[4]hoisted: lifted

Three fingers poked up under the cloth.

"Can you say it?" the barber asked.

"He's very shy," the boy's mother said. "But he can say it. He knows. He's three, aren't you, Robbie?" The boy nodded.

The barber twirled the chair around twice. "Well, he certainly is handsome. Aren't you, Robbie? Aren't you the handsomest kid in all Five Oaks?"

The boy said, "No," and looked at the floor. He smiled for a split second, and, just as quickly as the smile had appeared, it vanished.

"Everyone's handsome at three," the barber said. "It's later that they aren't. Louise, how do you want his hair cut?"

"Sort of normal," she said. "Sort of like a normal boy."

Harold nodded and began clipping around the boy's ears. His knees were trembling slightly and he had to lean against the chair to steady himself. He noticed that his scissors weren't quite steady, either, so he stopped for a moment. His face, and Robbie's, and Louise's, were reflected, in the usual way of barber shops, forty or fifty times, accordion-like, back into darkness between the two wall mirrors.

"How's George?" the barber asked.

"George? George is fine. George is always fine. He's the definition of fine. Except he's losing his hair. You should know. You cut it. Don't you two talk?"

"Yes," Harold said. "About the weather. And sports."

"Sports? You always hated sports," she said. "You told me."

"I'm a barber, Louise. I have to talk to these men about something."

"Well," Louise said, standing by the window, "you could talk to George about me."

"What would I say? I don't see you anymore,

except to wave. And I don't want to be curious, do I?" He stopped cutting the boy's hair to glance at her. She shrugged. "No, I do not talk to George about you. That's not even . . ." He thought of a word he never used. "Conceivable.⁵ That's not conceivable."

"Oh, you *could* say something about me. To him. But he wouldn't notice. He'd go right on sitting, having his hair cut, and not noticing."

Robbie squirmed, and Harold began to sing "Boris the Spider,"⁶ walking his fingers across the top of the boy's head. Robbie laughed and said, "No Boris." When he had settled down again, Harold bent to clip the hair at the back of the boy's neck.

"Robbie's hair color is the same as yours," Louise said, "and his eyes, too, the exact same. You know, sometimes I have these thoughts, when I'm lying in bed, late at night, next to George, and he's snoring, you know, asleep and ignoring me, and anyway, I'm looking at the way my toes poke up under the blankets, so there are two little peaks down there at the end of the bed, and I'm having these thoughts, and the only trouble with them is, they're tricky. You can't say them around George, you know?"

"Sort of," Harold said. She was as beautiful and as crazy as ever. His craziness, his wildness, had once been able to match hers, and then it could not. "Have you ever tried to say them?"

"I'm trying to say them now," Louise said. "You remember in junior high, when we had that math teacher, Mr. Powers—"

"He taught shop class."

"He did that too. Anyway, once in science club, one of our meetings when you weren't there, he said

---

⁵conceivable: able to be imagined
⁶"Boris the Spider": children's song

that maybe the universe was imaginary. That maybe it was all made up. And that it could be a *thought* in someone's head. Or, maybe it was a *trick*, sort of like a practical joke."

"What are you saying, Louise?"

"You're so handsome, Harold, no wonder I fell in love with you. But you're so *mild*. You never took me anywhere. You never even drove me out of this town. You talked softly and you had nice hands but you didn't spirit me away.[7] That was the one thing you had to do, and you never did it. You never even took me to a movie. Of course there was George by then, but you see what I'm getting at."

"Oh, God, Louise," he said. "For God's sake."

"But that's it," she said, "that's what I'm *saying*. I'm not blaming you. You never took me away because I was married to George, that was the first thing, and the second thing was, you were yourself. Mild. A very very mild and pleasant-feeling man who never did anything except cut hair. Who couldn't take me away because he just couldn't, that's all. And that's what I mean about the universe. Those are my thoughts, when I'm lying awake at night."

"Your thoughts."

"Yes."

"I don't get the part about the universe." He was finishing up on Robbie's hair, trimming along the sides, going quickly so the boy wouldn't have to sit much longer. The fine, blondish curls fell over his fingers onto the floor.

"The universe, Harold, is a practical joke."

"On who?"

"Why, on us, of course. They put it together to be a joke on us."

---

[7]spirit away: carry off

"No, they didn't." He let himself take another glance at her. Her face had its customary intensity,[8] which made her beautiful no matter what her thoughts were. Harold lightly brushed the hair away from the back of the boy's neck. "It's too complicated to be a joke. Let's get a look at you, young man." He swiveled the chair around so that he was face to face with Robbie. "He looks very good. Like a proud little boy." He touched the fingers of his right hand to his own lips, and then lightly placed the fingers on the side of the boy's cheek. A shiver ran down his back.

"I saw that," she said.

"What?"

"Don't think I didn't see it."

Harold lowered the chair, pulled the cloth away from around the boy, and flicked out the hairs onto the floor. The boy jumped down and went to the window.

"Up there," the boy said. At that moment one of Harold's regular customers, a teacher in the high school named Saul Bernstein, walked into the shop, ringing the bell over the door.

"Hey, Harold," he said. "See the balloon?" He pointed outside, toward the sky. Down at the other end of the main street a hot air balloon with an enormous red tulip painted on its side was floating in a northerly direction just above treetop level toward Harold's barbershop. "Well, hello," he said to the boy.

The boy turned to look at Saul. "Hi," he said. Meanwhile, the boy's mother was reaching into her purse for money. From her pocketbook she drew out a ten-dollar bill and handed it to Harold.

"You can't give me money, Louise," he said quietly, handing it back to her. "You just can't." Saul watched the two of them for a moment, then walked to

---

[8]customary intensity: usual expressiveness

the back of the barbershop and began to search through the old copies of *Argosy* and *Sports Illustrated*.

By now, both the boy and his mother had their spring coats on. Louise touched Harold once on the arm, then turned toward the window. "It's dropping something," she said. "Little sheets of paper."

"Those are the coupons," Harold said, rubbing his hand across his eyes. "Like I told you. The whole thing's a promotion for Five Oaks businesses. We're trying—" He seemed to lose his thought for a moment. "We're trying to keep the businesses prosperous."[9] He laughed, a faint and unhappy sound deep in his throat. "Two dollars off a haircut if you use the coupon before May first."

"Well," Louise said, "we'll just have to go out, Robbie and me, and search up and down the street till we find one of your coupons, Harold, and that way, the next time we come, we won't have to spend George's money at full price."

Harold didn't say anything.

"We'll come back," Louise said, "because I love the haircut you gave Robbie, it's just wonderful how he looks now, and I want you to be his barber. I don't mean just now; I mean from now on. Won't that be nice? Every month, you can cut Robbie's hair."

Harold seemed to nod at the floor.

"Mom?" the boy said. "Go out now?" His mother smiled, opened the door for him, and, as soon as he was out on the sidewalk, she walked over to Harold and kissed him on the cheek.

"Tulip Days," she said. "What a good way to welcome in the spring." She brushed a bit of her son's hair off Harold's shoulders and then turned to go. "See you," she said. "And God bless you, and I mean that."

---

[9]prosperous: financially successful

When the bell rang again, announcing her exit, Saul put down the magazine he had been reading and walked over to the window, taking his time. Outside, white coupons were fluttering down out of the sky and landing on the sidewalk and in the street; some of the cars going by had their windshield wipers on. Louise's boy stood next to a parking meter in the snowstorm of paper, one coupon stuck to his forehead and another lodged[10] in his shirt at the back of his neck. His mouth was open, as if he hoped a coupon would drop into it. His mother had turned to walk down the street; she was checking in the gutters and poking at the papers with the toe of her boot.

"You know," Saul said, standing beside Harold at the front of the window, "I love this town. They do this promotion, even remember to do it on Saturday, but then they forget about publicizing[11] it, so no one's here, almost, except the usual layabouts[12] like me, and a few others like that lady out there, grabbing up those coupons. What's the matter, Harold, you feeling a little faint?"

For a moment the barber had leaned forward, and he had had to reach out and touch the sill to straighten up. "I'm fine," he said. "I had a touch of the flu. But that was last month. I just feel a little bit of it now and then."

"Must be what screwed up your bowling last week," Saul said. "Another night like that, and we'll have to drum you out[13] of the league. Ha." Saul had a laugh which was not a laugh, but a spoken word, which he sometimes put at the end of his sentences.

---

[10]lodged: stuck
[11]publicizing: making well known
[12]layabouts: lazy people
[13]drum out: push out

"You guys running these businesses are going to have to think of something else next year instead of dumping all these trashy discount slips out of a hot air balloon onto the street. It's not good for business. It's too weird. I don't care if it *is* Tulip Days."

"Saul, you want your hair cut, or what?"

"A trim. The usual trim so I don't look like a wildman and give all the other Jews in this town a bad name."

"Okay," Harold said. "I think I can do that. But you got to sit down in the chair."

"Torture by Mr. Harold of Paris," Saul said, settling himself in the chair. "And don't do any of that funny stuff with the hair dryer. That was a cute kid, that boy whose hair you just cut. You did a nice job. A real sweetie, that kid was. Did I tell you Patsy is pregnant? My wife? Patsy? Harold? Hello? Hello?"

Harold was standing behind Saul, a pair of scissors in his right hand. He was staring at the floor and holding onto the chair with his other hand.

"Harold?"

"What?"

"Harold," Saul said. "Maybe you need a little air."

"Yes."

"Such as having the door open."

"Yes."

"Buck up, Harold. Life goes on. Listen, you want to close the shop for a minute and go out for a beer? Want to do a bit of basketball down at the high school? I've got the keys, Harold, keys to the gym. You could practice that lousy lay-up of yours, and that jump shot. How about that?"

"That would . . . yes," Harold said. He was looking at himself in the mirrors, his reflections curving back into darkness.

"No more of this," Saul said, getting out of the chair and taking the cloth off from around his neck.

"No more snipping hair this morning. Come on, Harold, we'll go have lunch." He stood at the door and turned the sign so that it read CLOSED. "Let's go."

"I should stay. It's supposed to be a big business day."

"Come on, Harold. A break. To relax."

"All right." He took off his smock and went over to the coat rack for his jacket. "You know," he said suddenly, "the coupons and the hot air balloon were my idea. They were all my idea. The things I think of doing. Now it's all on the street, but we forgot about the wind. Imagine. It's spring, but we forgot about that."

"It was a good idea, Harold, a *good* idea, and very original." They went out to the sidewalk, and Harold closed the door behind him and locked it. Coupons were swirling in circle patterns and now stuck against his shoes. "It's a day of discounts," Saul said. "Everything's discounted today. The world is forty percent off. We should take advantage."

"Sun's out," Harold said.

"My point exactly." Saul bent down toward the gutter and gathered up two handfuls of coupons. "Bargains galore.[14] What should we do with all these coupons, Harold?"

"Make them fly," Harold said.

"Anything you say." Saul threw a fistful of papers up into the air, and as they fell, Harold thought of the one time when he *had* taken Louise out for dinner, one weekend when George was gone. She must have forgotten. They had driven to a seafood restaurant thirty miles away, in Bay City, and Louise had ordered whitefish. All during the meal, she had held his hand.

---

[14]galore: plentiful

He hadn't noticed how awkward it had been, hadn't even thought about it until later, when he had patiently reimagined the dinner, minute by minute. The light from the candle had made her hair shine with a slightly reddish glow; the curls, and the way they fell over her shoulders, made him think that any kind of future might be possible. But they didn't talk about their future. Instead, they sat there describing each other, the small details each one liked. He had thought, in that moment, that he was perfectly happy, and, thinking of that moment now, Harold smiled and reached out to touch Saul's shoulder.

"Did you know that woman?" Harold asked.

"No, Harold, I never did."

"I knew her once."

"I know that." He reached for the barber's sleeve. "Hamburger time," he said, walking up the street toward the diner.

REFLECT ·································

What is the first clue in the story that tells you Harold and Louise were once close?

How did Harold used to feel about Louise? Have his feelings changed?

How did Louise used to feel about Harold? How does she feel now? What does she think of her husband?

Who is Robbie's father? What clues in the story tell you this?

How much does Saul know about Harold and Louise's former relationship? How can you tell?

Why did the author include so much description of the hot-air balloon and the Tulip Days promotion?

WRITE ································

Though Harold and Louise loved each other, personality differences pulled them apart. What do you think they said to each other when they broke up? Write a conversation in which they discuss their differences.

Harold and Louise were in school together. Based on their personalities as adults, imagine what they were like as teenagers. Write a brief description that might have appeared next to each one's picture in their high school yearbook. What kind of personality did each have? What clubs or organizations did each belong to? What were each person's plans for the future?

The story is told by an outsider—an unnamed
person who doesn't participate in the action.
Imagine how the story would change if it were told
by Louise's husband. Write the story of Louise and
Harold's relationship from George's point of view. If
you want, use the following beginning to get started.

> Louise and Harold think that I don't
> know about their past relationship, but
> I know all about it. I first found out
> when . . .

Has your understanding of a poem ever changed over several readings? Try reading "Unfolding Bud" two or three times before you form an opinion. As you read, compare your experience reading poetry with the poet's.

Unfolding Bud

Naoshi Koriyama

One is amazed
By a water-lily bud
Unfolding
With each passing day,
Taking on a richer color
And new dimensions.[1]

One is not amazed,
At a first glance,[2]
By a poem,
Which is as tight-closed
As a tiny bud.

Yet one is surprised
To see the poem
Gradually unfolding,
Revealing[3] its rich inner self,
As one reads it
Again
And over again.

---

[1]dimensions: size and shape
[2]glance: quick look
[3]revealing: showing

REFLECT ·

What natural event is described in the first stanza, or part, of the poem? Why does the speaker describe the event as "amazing"?

What comparison is made in the second stanza? In the third?

Do you think the comparisons are effective? Why or why not?

WRITE ·

Imagine that you are in charge of choosing poems for a new book. Would you include "Unfolding Bud"? Write a note explaining why you would—or wouldn't—put the poem in your book.

The speaker in the poem is amazed by a small, everyday event. Write about a common event that amazes you.

Just as someone's understanding of a poem can deepen, so can someone's understanding of another person. Write about a time when your first impression of someone changed as you got to know the person better.

Jerome Witkin, *Elvina Alderman*, 1986, oil on canvas
Collection of Georgia and Nathan Kramer, White Plains, New York

Several episodes of "Alfred Hitchcock Presents" were based on Henry Slesar's stories. If the show is rerun in your area, watch for the episode based on the story below.

Do you like mystery stories? When you watch a mystery unfolding in a movie or a TV show, do you try to solve it? In the mystery story that follows, Mr. Waterbury wants very much to buy a particular house. As you read, ask yourself why he wants the house so much—and why the owner has set the price so high.

The Right Kind of House

Henry Slesar

The automobile that was stopping in front of Aaron Hacker's real estate office had a New York license plate. Aaron didn't need to see the white rectangle to know that its owner was new to the elm-shaded streets of Ivy Corners. It was a red convertible; there was nothing else like it in town.

The man got out of the car.

"Sally," Hacker said to the bored young lady at the only other desk. There was a paperbound book propped in her typewriter, and she was chewing something dreamily.

"Yes, Mr. Hacker?"

"Seems to be a customer. Think we oughta look busy?" He put the question mildly.

"Sure, Mr. Hacker!" She smiled brightly, removed the book, and slipped a blank sheet of paper into the machine. "What shall I type?"

"Anything, anything!" Aaron scowled.

It looked like a customer, all right. The man was heading straight for the glass door, and there was a folded newspaper in his right hand. Aaron described him later as heavy-set. Actually, he was fat. He wore a colorless suit of lightweight material, and the perspiration had soaked clean through the fabric to leave large, damp circles around his arms. He might have been fifty, but he had all his hair, and it was dark and curly. The skin of his face was flushed[1] and hot, but the narrow eyes remained clear and frosty-cold.

He came through the doorway, glanced toward the rattling sound of the office typewriter, and then nodded at Aaron.

"Mr. Hacker?"

"Yes, sir," Aaron smiled. "What can I do for you?"

The fat man waved the newspaper. "I looked you up in the real estate section."

"Yep. Take an ad every week. I use the *Times*, too, now and then. Lot of city people interested in a town like ours. Mr.—"

"Waterbury," the man said. He plucked a white cloth out of his pocket and mopped his face. "Hot today."

"Unusually hot," Aaron answered. "Doesn't often get so hot in our town. Mean temperature's around seventy-eight in the summer. We got the lake, you know. Isn't that right, Sally?" The girl was too absorbed to hear him. "Well. Won't you sit down, Mr. Waterbury?"

"Thank you." The fat man took the proffered[2] chair, and sighed. "I've been driving around. Thought

---

[1]flushed: red
[2]proffered: suggested

I'd look the place over before I came here. Nice little town."

"Yes, we like it. Cigar?" He opened a box on his desk.

"No, thank you. I really don't have much time, Mr. Hacker. Suppose we get right down to business."

"Suits me, Mr. Waterbury." He looked toward the clacking noise and frowned. *"Sally!"*

"Yes, Mr. Hacker?"

"Cut out the darn racket."

"Yes, Mr. Hacker." She put her hands in her lap, and stared at the meaningless jumble of letters she had drummed on the paper.

"Now, then," Aaron said. "Was there any place in particular you were interested in, Mr. Waterbury?"

"As a matter of fact, yes. There was a house at the edge of town, across the way from an old building. Don't know what kind of building—deserted."

"Ice-house,"[3] Aaron said. "Was it a house with pillars?"

"Yes. That's the place. Do you have it listed? I thought I saw a 'for sale' sign, but I wasn't sure."

Aaron shook his head, and chuckled dryly. "Yep, we got it listed all right." He flipped over a loose-leaf book, and pointed to a typewritten sheet. "You won't be interested for long."

"Why not?"

He turned the book around. "Read it for yourself." The fat man did so.

AUTHENTIC COLONIAL. 8 rooms, two baths, automatic oil furnace, large porches, trees and shrubbery. Near shopping, schools. $175,000.

---

[3]ice-house: warehouse where ice was stored in the days before refrigerators

"Still interested?"

The man stirred uncomfortably. "Why not? Something wrong with it?"

"Well." Aaron scratched his temple. "If you really like this town, Mr. Waterbury—I mean, if you really want to settle here, I got any number of places that'd suit you better."

"Now, just a minute!" The fat man looked indignant. "What do you call this? I'm asking you about this colonial house. You want to sell it, or don't you?"

"Do I?" Aaron chuckled. "Mister, I've had that property on my hands for five years. There's nothing I'd rather collect a commission[4] on only my luck just ain't that good."

"What do you mean?"

"I mean, you won't buy. That's what I mean. I keep the listing on my books just for the sake of old Sadie Grimes. Otherwise, I wouldn't waste the space. Believe me."

"I don't get you."

"Then let me explain." He took out a cigar, but just to roll it in his fingers. "Old Mrs. Grimes put her place up for sale five years ago, when her son died. She gave me the job of selling it. I didn't want the job—no, sir. I told her that to her face. The old place just ain't worth the kind of money she's asking. I mean, heck! The old place ain't even worth *fifty* thousand!"

The fat man swallowed. "Fifty? And she wants one-seventy-five?"

"That's right. Don't ask me why. It's a real old house. Oh, I don't mean one of those solid-as-a-rock

---

[4]commission: fee

old houses. I mean *old*. Never been de-termited.[5] Some
of the beams will be going in the next couple of years.
Basement's full of water half the time. Upper floor
leans to the right about nine inches. And the grounds
are a mess."

"Then why does she ask so much?"

Aaron shrugged. "Don't ask me. Sentiment,
maybe. Been in her family since the Revolution, something like that."

The fat man studied the floor. "That's too bad,"
he said. "Too bad!" He looked up at Aaron, and smiled
sheepishly. "And I kinda liked the place. It was—I
don't know how to explain it—the *right* kind of
house."

"I know what you mean. It's a friendly old place.
A good buy at fifty thousand. But one-seventy-five?"
He laughed. "I think I know Sadie's reasoning, though.
You see, she doesn't have much money. Her son was
supporting her, doing well in the city. Then he died,
and she knew that it was sensible to sell. But she
couldn't bring herself to part with the old place. So she
put a price tag so big that *nobody* would come near it.
That eased her conscience." He shook his head sadly.
"It's a strange world, ain't it?"

"Yes," Waterbury said distantly.

Then he stood up. "Tell you what, Mr. Hacker.
Suppose I drive out to see Mrs. Grimes? Suppose I talk
to her about it, get her to change her price."

"You're fooling yourself, Mr. Waterbury. I've been
trying for five years."

"Who knows? Maybe if somebody *else* tried—"

Aaron Hacker spread his palms. "Who knows, is
right. It's a strange world, Mr. Waterbury. If you're

---

[5]de-termited: had the termites (wood-eating insects)
removed

willing to go to the trouble, I'll be only too happy to
lend a hand."

"Good. Then I'll leave now."

"Fine! You just let me ring Sadie Grimes. I'll tell
her you're on your way."

Waterbury drove slowly through the quiet streets.
The shade trees that lined the avenues cast peaceful
dappled[6] shadows on the hood of the convertible. The
powerful motor beneath it operated in whispers, so he
could hear the fitful chirpings of the birds overhead.

He reached the home of Sadie Grimes without
once passing another moving vehicle. He parked his
car beside the rotted picket fence that faced the house
like a row of disorderly sentries.

The lawn was a jungle of weeds and crabgrass,
and the columns that rose from the front porch were
entwined with creepers.[7]

There was a hand knocker on the door. He
pumped it twice.

The woman who responded was short and plump.
Her white hair was vaguely purple in spots, and the
lines in her face descended downward toward her
small, stubborn chin. She wore a heavy wool cardi-
gan,[8] despite the heat.

"You must be Mr. Waterbury," she said. "Aaron
Hacker said you were coming."

"Yes." The fat man smiled. "How do you do, Mrs.
Grimes?"

"Well as I can expect. I suppose you want to
come in?"

"Awfully hot out here." He chuckled.

---

[6]dappled: covered with dark patches
[7]creepers: vines
[8]cardigan: type of sweater

"Mm. Well, come in then. I've put some lemonade in the ice-box. Only don't expect me to bargain with you, Mr. Waterbury. I'm not that kind of person."

"Of course not," the man said winningly, and followed her inside.

It was dark and cool. The window shades were opaque,[9] and they had been drawn. They entered a square parlor with heavy, baroque[10] furniture shoved unimaginatively against every wall. The only color in the room was in the faded hues[11] of the tasseled rug that lay in the center of the bare floor.

The old woman headed straight for a rocker, and sat motionless, her wrinkled hands folded sternly.

"Well?" she said. "If you have anything to say, Mr. Waterbury, I suggest you say it."

The fat man cleared his throat. "Mrs. Grimes, I've just spoken with your real estate agent—"

"I know all that," she snapped. "Aaron's a fool. All the more for letting you come here with the notion of changing my mind. I'm too old for changing my mind, Mr. Waterbury."

"Er—well, I don't know if that was my intention, Mrs. Grimes. I thought we'd just—talk a little."

She leaned back, and the rocker groaned. "Talk's free. Say what you like."

"Yes." He mopped his face again, and shoved the handkerchief only halfway back into his pocket. "Well, let me put it this way, Mrs. Grimes. I'm a business-man—a bachelor. I've worked for a long time, and I've

---

[9]opaque: blocking out all light
[10]baroque: ornately carved
[11]hues: colors

made a fair amount of money. Now I'm ready to retire—preferably, somewhere quiet. I like Ivy Corners. I passed through here some years back, on my way to—er, Albany. I thought, one day, I might like to settle here."

"So?"

"So, when I drove through your town today, and saw this house—I was enthused. It just seemed—right for me."

"I like it too, Mr. Waterbury. That's why I'm asking a fair price for it."

Waterbury blinked. "Fair price? You'll have to admit, Mrs. Grimes, these days a house like this shouldn't cost more than—"

"That's enough!" the old woman cried. "I told you, Mr. Waterbury—I don't want to sit here all day and argue with you. If you won't pay my price, then we can forget all about it."

"But, Mrs. Grimes—"

"Good *day*, Mr. Waterbury!"

She stood up, indicating that he was expected to do the same.

But he didn't. "Wait a moment, Mrs. Grimes," he said, "just a moment. I know it's crazy, but—all right. I'll pay what you want."

She looked at him for a long moment. "Are you sure, Mr. Waterbury?"

"Positive! I've enough money. If that's the only way you'll have it, that's the way it'll be."

She smiled thinly. "I think that lemonade'll be cold enough. I'll bring you some—and then I'll tell you something about this house."

He was mopping his brow when she returned with the tray. He gulped at the frosty yellow beverage greedily.

"This house," she said, easing back in her rocker, "has been in my family since eighteen hundred and two. It was built some fifteen years before that. Every member of the family, except my son, Michael, was born in the bedroom upstairs. I was the only rebel," she added raffishly.[12] "I had new-fangled[13] ideas about hospitals." Her eyes twinkled.

"I know it's not the most solid house in Ivy Corners. After I brought Michael home, there was a flood in the basement, and we never seemed to get it dry since. Aaron tells me there are termites, too, but I've never seen the pesky things. I love the old place, though; you understand."

"Of course," Waterbury said.

"Michael's father died when Michael was nine. It was hard times on us then. I did some needlework, and my own father had left me the small annuity which supports me today. Not in very grand style, but I manage. Michael missed his father, perhaps even more than I. He grew up to be—well, wild is the only word that comes to mind."

The fat man clucked, sympathetically.

"When he graduated from high school, Michael left Ivy Corners and went to the city. Against my wishes, make no mistake. But he was like so many young men; full of ambition, undirected ambition. I don't know what he did in the city. But he must have been successful—he sent me money regularly." Her eyes clouded. "I didn't see him for nine years."

"And," the man sighed, sadly.

"Yes, it wasn't easy for me. But it was even worse when Michael came home because, when he did, he was in trouble."

"Oh?"

---

[12]raffishly: with a devil-may-care attitude
[13]new-fangled: modern

"I didn't know how bad the trouble was. He showed up in the middle of the night, looking thinner and older than I could have believed possible. He had no luggage with him, only a small black suitcase. When I tried to take it from him, he almost struck me. Struck *me*—his own mother!

"I put him to bed myself, as if he was a little boy again. I could hear him crying out during the night.

"The next day, he told me to leave the house. Just for a few hours—he wanted to do something, he said. He didn't explain what. But when I returned that evening, I noticed that the little black suitcase was gone."

The fat man's eyes widened over the lemonade glass.

"What did it mean?" he asked.

"I didn't know then. But I found out soon—too terribly soon. That night, a man came to our house. I don't even know how he got in. I first knew when I heard voices in Michael's room. I went to the door, and tried to listen, tried to find out what sort of trouble my boy was in. But I heard only shouts and threats, and then . . ."

She paused, and her shoulders sagged.

"And a shot," she continued, "a gunshot. When I went into the room, I found the bedroom window open, and the stranger gone. And Michael—he was on the floor. He was dead."

The chair creaked.

"That was five years ago," she said. "Five long years. It was a while before I realized what had happened. The police told me the story. Michael and this other man had been involved in a crime, a serious crime. They had stolen many, many thousands of dollars.

"Michael had taken that money, and run off with it, wanting to keep it all for himself. He hid it somewhere in this house—to this very day I don't know where. Then the other man came looking for my son, came to collect his share. When he found the money gone, he—he killed my boy."

She looked up. "That's when I put the house up for sale, at $175,000. I knew that, someday, my son's killer would return. Someday, he would want this house at any price. All I had to do was wait until I found the man willing to pay much too much for an old lady's house."

She rocked gently.

Waterbury put down the empty glass and licked his lips, his eyes no longer focusing, his head rolling loosely on his shoulders.

"*Ugh!*" he said. "This lemonade is bitter."

REFLECT ································

According to Mr. Hacker, the real estate man, why is Sadie Grimes asking such a high price for her run-down old house? What is the *real* reason?

Though Sadie Grimes and the other people in Ivy Corners don't know it, Mr. Waterbury once knew Sadie's son. Describe Michael Grimes and Mr. Waterbury's secret past.

Why is Mr. Waterbury willing to pay such a high price for Sadie Grimes's run-down old house?

What do you think will happen to Mr. Waterbury? To Sadie Grimes?

In your opinion, is "The Right Kind of House" a mystery story, a revenge tale, or both? Explain why you feel as you do.

WRITE ································

Imagine that you are making a movie based on "The Right Kind of House." What actors would you hire to play the following roles? Give reasons for each of your choices.

- Aaron Hacker
- Sally the secretary
- Sadie Grimes
- Mr. Waterbury

Imagine that you are selling your house or renting the apartment you live in. Write an ad that makes the place sound as attractive as possible. (Stick to the facts, but make them appealing.) Then describe the place in a way that would keep anyone from wanting to buy it.

The last lines of "The Right Kind of House" are as follows:

> Waterbury put down the empty glass and licked his lips, his eyes no longer focusing, his head rolling loosely on his shoulders.
>
> "*Ugh!*" he said. "This lemonade is bitter."

What happened just after the point where the story ends? Write a new ending that picks up where the present one leaves off.

Have you ever felt frightened when you were home alone at night? As you read the poem below, try to imagine what it's like to be old and weak and lonely—and to feel that fear all the time.

Old Couple

Charles Simic

They're waiting to be murdered,
Or evicted. Soon
They expect to have nothing to eat.
As far as I know, they never go out.

A vicious pain's coming, they think.
It will start in the head
And spread down to the bowels.
They'll be carried off on stretchers, howling.

In the meantime, they watch the street
From their fifth floor window.
It has rained, and now it looks
Like it's going to snow a little.

I see him get up to lower the shades.
If their window stays dark,
I know that his hand has reached hers
Just as she was about to turn on the lights.

REFLECT ······························

What is the old couple afraid of? Do you think the fears are reasonable?

Why does the old couple watch the street? What might the husband and wife be watching for?

Why does the old man keep his wife from turning on the lights?

What emotion do you feel most strongly when you read the poem? What do you think the speaker is feeling?

WRITE ······························

Imagine that you are a TV reporter working on a special show about the problems of the elderly. Write a list of questions that you could use to interview the old couple in the poem.

The old couple is afraid of many things. Describe one of your fears.

Imagine that you live in the old couple's neighborhood. Write a letter to the editor of the local newspaper. Explain what you think should be done to make older people in the community feel safe.

Romare Bearden, *Black Manhattan*, 1969, collage
Courtesy of the Estate of Romare Bearden

Have you ever been forced to swallow your pride in order to get the help you needed? The mother and daughter in the following story find themselves in just such a situation. As you read, ask yourself what facts of life the title refers to.

Getting the Facts of Life

Paulette Childress White

The August morning was ripening into a day that promised to be a burner.[1] By the time we'd walked three blocks, dark patches were showing beneath Momma's arms, and inside tennis shoes thick with white polish, my feet were wet against the cushions. I was beginning to regret how quickly I'd volunteered to go.

"Dog. My feet are getting mushy," I complained.

"You should've wore socks," Momma said, without looking my way or slowing down.

I frowned. In 1961, nobody wore socks with tennis shoes. It was bare legs, Bermuda shorts and a sleeveless blouse. Period.

Momma was chubby but she could really walk. She walked the same way she washed clothes—up-and-down, up-and-down until she was done. She didn't believe in taking breaks.

This was my first time going to the welfare office with Momma. After breakfast, before we'd had time to scatter, she corralled[2] everyone old enough to consider

---

[1]burner: very hot
[2]corralled: gathered together

and announced in her serious-business voice that someone was going to the welfare office with her this morning. Cries went up.

Junior had his papers to do. Stella was going swimming at the high school. Dennis was already pulling the *Free Press*³ wagon across town every first Wednesday to get the surplus food—like that.

"You want clothes for school, don't you?" That landed.⁴ School opened in two weeks.

"I'll go," I said.

"Who's going to baby-sit if Minerva goes?" Momma asked.

Stella smiled and lifted her golden nose. "I will," she said. "I'd rather baby-sit than do *that*."

That should have warned me. Anything that would make Stella offer to baby-sit had to be bad.

A small cheer probably went up among my younger brothers in the back rooms where I was not too secretly known as "The Witch" because of the criminal licks⁵ I'd learned to give on my rise to power. I was twelve, third oldest under Junior and Stella, but I had long established myself as first in command among the kids. I was chief baby-sitter, biscuit-maker and broom-wielder.⁶ Unlike Stella, who'd begun her development at ten, I still had my girl's body and wasn't anxious to have that changed. What would it mean but a loss of power? I liked things just the way they were. My interest in bras was even less than my interest in boys, and that was limited to keeping my brothers—who seemed destined for wildness—from taking over completely.

---

³*Free Press*: Detroit newspaper
⁴landed: made an impression
⁵licks: punches
⁶broom-wielder: sweeper

Even before we left, Stella had Little Stevie Wonder turned up on the radio in the living room, and suspicious jumping-bumping sounds were beginning in the back. They'll tear the house down, I thought, following Momma out the door.

We turned at Salliotte, the street that would take us straight up to Jefferson Avenue where the welfare office was. Momma's face was pinking in the heat, and I was huffing to keep up. From here, it was seven more blocks on the colored side, the railroad tracks, five blocks on the white side and there you were. We'd be cooked.

"Is the welfare office near the Harbor Show?" I asked. I knew the answer, I just wanted some talk.

"Across the street."

"Umm. Glad it's not way down Jefferson somewhere."

Nothing. Momma didn't talk much when she was outside. I knew that the reason she wanted one of us along when she had far to go was not for company but so she wouldn't have to walk by herself. I could understand that. To me, walking alone was like being naked or deformed—everyone seemed to look at you harder and longer. With Momma, the feeling was probably worse because you knew people were wondering if she were white, Indian maybe or really colored. Having one of us along, brown and clearly hers, probably helped define that. Still, it was like being a little parade, with Momma's pale skin and straight brown hair turning heads like the clang of cymbals. Especially on the colored side.

"Well," I said, "here we come to the bad part."

Momma gave a tiny laugh.

Most of Salliotte was a business street, with Old West-looking storefronts and some office places that never seemed to open. Ecorse, hinged onto southwest Detroit like a clothes closet, didn't seem to take itself seriously. There were lots of empty fields, some of which folks down the residential streets turned into vegetable gardens every summer. And there was this block where the Moonflower Hotel raised itself to three stories over the poolroom and Beaman's drug-store. Here, bad boys and drunks made their noise and did an occasional stabbing. Except for the cars that lined both sides of the block, only one side was busy—the other bordered a field of weeds. We walked on the safe side.

If you were a woman or a girl over twelve, walk-ing this block—even on the safe side—could be pain-ful. They usually hollered at you and never mind what they said. Today, because it was hot and early, we made it by with only one weak *Hey baby* from a drunk sitting in the poolroom door.

"Hey baby yourself," I said but not too loudly, pushing my flat chest out and stabbing my eyes in his direction.

"Minerva girl, you better watch your mouth with grown men like that," Momma said, her eyes catching me up in real warning though I could see that she was holding down a smile.

"Well, he can't do nothing to me when I'm with you, can he?" I asked, striving to match the rise and fall of her black pumps.[7]

She said nothing. She just walked on, churning away under a sun that clearly meant to melt us. From here to the tracks it was mostly gardens. It felt like the Dixie Peach[8] I'd used to help water-wave my hair was sliding down with the sweat on my face, and my throat

---

[7]pumps: women's low-cut shoes
[8]Dixie Peach: brand of hair oil

was tight with thirst. Boy, did I want a pop. I looked at the last little store before we crossed the tracks without bothering to ask.

Across the tracks, there were no stores and no gardens. It was shady, and the grass was June green. Perfect-looking houses sat in unfenced spaces far back from the street. We walked these five blocks without a word. We just looked and hurried to get through it. I was beginning to worry about the welfare office in earnest. A fool could see that in this part of Ecorse, things got serious.

We had been on welfare for almost a year. I didn't have any strong feelings about it—my life went on pretty much the same. It just meant watching the mail for a check instead of Daddy getting paid, and occasional visits from a social worker that I'd always managed to miss. For Momma and whoever went with her, it meant this walk to the office and whatever went on there that made everyone hate to go. For Daddy, it seemed to bring the most change. For him, it meant staying away from home more than when he was working and a reason not to answer the phone.

At Jefferson, we turned left and there it was, halfway down the block. The Department of Social Services. I discovered some strong feelings. That fine name meant nothing. This was the welfare. The place for poor people. People who couldn't or wouldn't take care of themselves. Now I was going to face it, and suddenly I thought what I knew the others had thought, *What if I see someone I know?* I wanted to run back all those blocks to home.

I looked at Momma for comfort, but her face was closed and her mouth looked locked.

Inside, the place was gray. There were rows of long benches like church pews facing each other across a middle aisle that led to a central desk. Beyond the benches and the desk, four hallways led off to a maze[9] of partitioned[10] offices. In opposite corners, huge fans hung from the ceiling, humming from side to side, blowing the heavy air for a breeze.

Momma walked to the desk, answered some questions, was given a number and told to take a seat. I followed her through, trying not to see the waiting people—as though that would keep them from seeing me.

Gradually, as we waited, I took them all in. There was no one there that I knew, but somehow they all looked familiar. Or maybe I only thought they did, because when your eyes connected with someone's, they didn't quickly look away and they usually smiled. They were mostly women and children, and a few low-looking men. Some of them were white, which surprised me. I hadn't expected to see them in there.

Directly in front of the bench where we sat, a little girl with blond curls was trying to handle a bottle of Coke. Now and then, she'd manage to turn herself and the bottle around and watch me with big gray eyes that seemed to know quite well how badly I wanted a pop. I thought of asking Momma for fifteen cents so I could get one from the machine in the back but I was afraid she'd still say no so I just kept planning more and more convincing ways to ask. Besides, there was a water fountain near the door if I could make myself rise and walk to it.

We waited three hours. White ladies dressed like secretaries kept coming out to call numbers, and people on the benches would get up and follow down a hall. Then more people came in to replace them. I drank water from the fountain three times and was ready to put my feet up on the bench before us—the

---

[9]maze: confusing network
[10]partitioned: divided by walls

little girl with the Coke and her momma got called—
by the time we heard Momma's number.

"You wait here," Momma said as I rose with her.

I sat down with a plop.

The lady with the number looked at me. Her face
reminded me of the librarian's at Bunch school.
Looked like she never cracked a smile. "Let her come,"
she said.

"She can wait here," Momma repeated, weakly.

"It's OK. She can come in. Come on," the lady
insisted at me.

I hesitated, knowing that Momma's face was telling me to sit.

"Come on," the woman said.

Momma said nothing.

I got up and followed them into the maze. We
came to a small room where there was a desk and
three chairs. The woman sat behind the desk and we
before it.

For a while, no one spoke. The woman studied a
folder open before her, brows drawn together. On the
wall behind her there was a calendar with one heavy
black line drawn slantwise through each day of August, up to the twenty-first. That was today.

"Mrs. Blue, I have a notation[11] here that Mr. Blue
has not reported to the department on his efforts to
obtain[12] employment since the sixteenth of June. Before that, it was the tenth of April. You understand that
department regulations require that he report monthly
to this office, do you not?" Eyes brown as a wren's[13]
belly came up at Momma.

"Yes," Momma answered, sounding as small as
I felt.

---

[11]notation: note
[12]obtain: get
[13]wren: type of bird

"Can you explain his failure to do so?"

Pause. "He's been looking. He says he's been looking."

"That may be. However, his failure to report those efforts here is my only concern."

Silence.

"We cannot continue with your case as it now stands if Mr. Blue refuses to comply[14] with departmental regulations. He is still residing[15] with the family, is he not?"

"Yes, he is. I've been reminding him to come in . . . he said he would."

"Well, he hasn't. Regulations are that any able-bodied man, head-of-household and receiving assistance who neglects to report to this office any effort to obtain work for a period of sixty days or more is to be cut off for a minimum of three months, at which time he may reapply. As of this date, Mr. Blue is over sixty days delinquent,[16] and officially, I am obliged to close the case and direct you to other sources of aid."

"What is that?"

"Aid to Dependent Children would be the only source available to you. Then, of course, you would not be eligible unless it was verified that Mr. Blue was no longer residing with the family."

Another silence. I stared into the gray steel front of the desk, everything stopped but my heart.

"Well, can you keep the case open until Monday? If he comes in by Monday?"

"According to my records, Mr. Blue failed to come in May and such an agreement was made then. In all, we allowed him a period of seventy days. You must

---

[14]comply: follow
[15]residing: living
[16]delinquent: tardy

understand that what happens in such cases as this is not wholly my decision." She sighed and watched Momma with hopeless eyes, tapping the soft end of her pencil on the papers before her. "Mrs. Blue, I will speak to my superiors on your behalf. I can allow you until Monday next . . . that's the"—she swung around to the calendar—"twenty-sixth of August, to get him in here."

"Thank you. He'll be in," Momma breathed. "Will I be able to get the clothing order today?"

Hands and eyes searched in the folder for an answer before she cleared her throat and tilted her face at Momma. "We'll see what we can do," she said, finally.

My back touched the chair. Without turning my head, I moved my eyes down to Momma's dusty feet and wondered if she could still feel them; my own were numb. I felt bodyless—there was only my face, which wouldn't disappear, and behind it, one word pinging against another in a buzz that made no sense. At home, we'd have the house cleaned by now, and I'd be waiting for the daily appearance of my best friend, Bernadine, so we could comb each other's hair or talk about stuck-up Evelyn and Brenda. Maybe Bernadine was already there, and Stella was teaching her to dance the bop.

Then I heard our names and ages—all eight of them—being called off like items in a grocery list.

"Clifford, Junior, age fourteen." She waited.

"Yes."

"Born? Give me the month and year."

"October 1946," Momma answered, and I could hear in her voice that she'd been through these questions before.

"Stella, age thirteen."

"Yes."

"Born?"

"November 1947."

"Minerva, age twelve." She looked at me. "This is Minerva?"

"Yes."

No. I thought, no, this is not Minerva. You can write it down if you want to, but Minerva is not here.

"Born?"

"December 1948."

The woman went on down the list, sounding more and more like Momma should be sorry or ashamed, and Momma's answers grew fainter and fainter. So this was welfare. I wondered how many times Momma had had to do this. Once before? Three times? Every time?

More questions. How many in school? Six. Who needs shoes? Everybody.

"Everybody needs shoes? The youngest two?"

"Well, they don't go to school . . . but they walk."

My head came up to look at Momma and the woman. The woman's mouth was left open. Momma didn't blink.

The brown eyes went down. "Our allowances are based on the median[17] costs for moderately[18] priced clothing at Sears, Roebuck." She figured on paper as she spoke. "That will mean thirty-four dollars for children over ten . . . thirty dollars for children under ten. It comes to one hundred ninety-eight dollars. I can allow eight dollars for two additional pairs of shoes."

"Thank you."

"You will present your clothing order to a salesperson at the store, who will be happy to assist you in your selections. Please be practical as further clothing requests will not be considered for a period of six

---

[17]median: average
[18]moderately: reasonably

months. In cases of necessity, however, requests for winter outerwear will be considered beginning November first."

Momma said nothing.

The woman rose and left the room.

For the first time, I shifted in the chair. Momma was looking into the calendar as though she could see through the pages to November first. Everybody needed a coat.

I'm never coming here again, I thought. If I do, I'll stay out front. Not coming back in here. Ever again.

She came back and sat behind her desk. "Mrs. Blue, I must make it clear that, regardless of my feelings, I will be forced to close your case if your husband does not report to this office by Monday, the twenty-sixth. Do you understand?"

"Yes. Thank you. He'll come. I'll see to it."

"Very well." She held a paper out to Momma.

We stood. Momma reached over and took the slip of paper. I moved toward the door.

"Excuse me, Mrs. Blue, but are you pregnant?"

"What?"

"I asked if you were expecting another child."

"Oh. No, I'm not," Momma answered, biting down on her lips.

"Well, I'm sure you'll want to be careful about a thing like that in your present situation."

"Yes."

I looked quickly to Momma's loose white blouse. We'd never known when another baby was coming until it was almost there.

"I suppose that eight children are enough for anyone," the woman said, and for the first time her face broke into a smile.

Momma didn't answer that. Somehow, we left the room and found our way out onto the street. We stood for a moment as though lost. My eyes followed Momma's up to where the sun was burning high. It was still there, blazing white against a cloudless blue. Slowly, Momma put the clothing order into her purse and snapped it shut. She looked around as if uncertain which way to go. I led the way to the corner. We turned. We walked the first five blocks.

I was thinking about how stupid I'd been a year ago, when Daddy lost his job. I'd been happy.

"You all better be thinking about moving to Indianapolis," he announced one day after work, looking like he didn't think much of it himself. He was a welder with the railroad company. He'd worked there for eleven years. But now, "Company's moving to Indianapolis," he said. "Gonna be gone by November. If I want to keep my job, we've got to move with it."

We didn't. Nobody wanted to move to Indianapolis—not even Daddy. Here, we had uncles, aunts and cousins on both sides. Friends. Everybody and everything we knew. Daddy could get another job. First came unemployment compensation. Then came welfare. Thank goodness for welfare, we said while we waited and waited for that job that hadn't yet come.

The problem was that Daddy couldn't take it. If something got repossessed or somebody took sick or something was broken or another kid was coming he'd carry on terribly until things got better—by which time things were always worse. He'd always been that way. So when the railroad left, he began to do everything wrong. Stayed out all hours. Drank and drank some more. When he was home, he was so grouchy we were afraid to squeak. Now when we saw him coming, we got lost. Even our friends ran for cover.

At the railroad tracks, we sped up. The tracks were as far across as a block was long. Silently, I counted the rails by the heat of the steel bars through my thin soles. On the other side, I felt something heavy rise up in my chest and I knew that I wanted to cry. I wanted to cry or run or kiss the dusty ground. The little houses with their sun scorched lawns and backyard gardens were mansions in my eyes. "Ohh, Ma . . . look at those collards!"[19]

"Umm-hummm," she agreed, and I knew that she saw it too.

"Wonder how they grew so big?"

"Cow dung,[20] probably. Big Poppa used to put cow dung out to fertilize the vegetable plots, and everything just grew like crazy. We used to get tomatoes this big"—she circled with her hands—"and don't talk about squash or melons."

"I bet y'all ate like rich people. Bet y'all had everything you could want."

"We sure did," she said. "We never wanted for anything when it came to food. And when the cash crops were sold, we could get whatever else that was needed. We never wanted for a thing."

"What about the time you and cousin Emma threw out the supper peas?"

"Oh! Did I tell you about that?" she asked. Then she told it all over again. I didn't listen. I watched her face and guarded her smile with a smile of my own.

We walked together, step for step. The sun was still burning, but we forgot to mind it. We talked about an Alabama girlhood in a time and place I'd never know. We talked about the wringer washer and how it could be fixed, because washing every day on a scrubboard was something Alabama could keep. We talked about how to get Daddy to the Department of Social Services.

---

[19]collards: leafy green vegetables
[20]dung: manure

Then we talked about having babies. She began to tell me things I'd never known, and the idea of womanhood blossomed in my mind like some kind of suffocating rose.

"Momma," I said, "I don't think I can be a woman."

"You can," she laughed. "And if you live, you will be. You gotta be some kind of woman."

"But it's hard," I said, "sometimes it must be hard."

"Umm-humm," she said, "sometimes it is hard."

When we got to the bad block, we crossed to Beaman's drugstore for two orange crushes. Then we walked right through the groups of men standing in the shadows of the poolroom and the Moonflower Hotel. Not one of them said a word to us. I supposed they could see in the way we walked that we weren't afraid. We'd been to the welfare office and back again. And the facts of life, fixed in our minds like the sun in the sky, were no burning mysteries.

REFLECT ····································

Why does Mrs. Blue want one of her children to go with her to the welfare office? Why does Minerva offer to go?

How does Minerva feel as she and her mother near the welfare office? Why does she feel this way?

Why does Mrs. Blue want Minerva to stay in the welfare office waiting room? Why doesn't Minerva obey her mother?

In your opinion, did the case worker at the welfare office treat Mrs. Blue fairly? Is there anything that you think the case worker should—or shouldn't— have done?

Why is "Getting the Facts of Life" a fitting title for the story?

WRITE ·································

What is Mrs. Blue like? Make a list of at least three words that describe her. After each word, name a time or times when she shows the quality. Use the following example as a model:

- Courageous—Mrs. Blue is courageous when she answers the case worker's embarrassing questions to help her family. Also, she is courageous when she walks past the men standing in front of the poolroom and the hotel.

Minerva and her mother grow closer as a result of their shared experience. Write about a time when you grew closer to a parent or other family member as a result of an experience you shared.

How did Minerva feel after the trip to the welfare office? Imagine that you are Minerva, and write a page in your diary describing your trip and what you learned as a result of it.

*Have you ever found yourself caught in
the middle between two people you love?
As you read, think about how you would
feel if you were in the son's place.*

My Father's Leaving

Ira Sadoff

When I came back, he was gone.
My mother was in the bathroom
crying, my sister in her crib
restless but asleep. The sun
was shining in the bay window,
the grass had just been cut.
No one mentioned the other woman,
nights he spent in that stranger's house.

I sat at my desk and wrote him a note.
When my mother saw his name on the sheet
of paper, she asked me to leave the house.
When she spoke, her voice was like a whisper
to someone else, her hand a weight
on my arm I could not feel.

In the evening, though, I opened the door
and saw a thousand houses just like ours.
I thought I was the one who was leaving,
and behind me I heard my mother's voice
asking me to stay. But I was thirteen
and wishing I were a man I listened
to no one, and no words from a woman
I loved were strong enough to make me stop.

REFLECT ··································

At the beginning of the poem, the father has just left home. Why did he leave?

In your opinion, is the father gone for good?

Why did the mother ask the son to leave when she saw the father's name on the note? Do you think she was being fair? Why or why not?

The son says that his mother's voice sounds like "a whisper to someone else." Why does her voice sound strange? Why can't the son feel the weight of her hand on his arm?

Why does the son ignore the mother when she asks him to stay?

WRITE ··································

What did the son write in the note to his father? Imagine that you are the son, and write the note.

What do you think happened after the end of the poem? Where did the speaker go? Did he return to his mother or go to live with his father? Imagine that you are the son, and write a page in your journal explaining where you went and how you felt.

Write about a time when you were the son's age and you did something—even though you knew it was a mistake—because you wanted to feel grown-up and independent.

William H. Johnson, *Woman in Calico*, 1944, oil on paperboard
National Museum of American Art, Washington, D.C.
Photograph: Art Resource, New York

Have you ever known someone who worked and sacrificed for an ungrateful loved one? Mary, the woman in the following story, is someone like that. The tale of how she finally got back at her husband is told by her best friend. The friend's way of speaking reflects the rural Southern setting of the story. Sometimes she uses the wrong words for what she means. Try reading the story out loud to understand what she is saying. As you read, ask yourself how you would feel if you were Mary.

$100 and Nothing!

J. California Cooper

Where we live is not a big town like some and not a little town like some, but somewhere in the middle, like a big little town. Things don't happen here very much like other places, but on the other hand, I guess they do. Just ever¹ once in awhile, you really pay tention² to what is going on around you. I seen something here really was something! Let me tell you!

Was a woman, friend of mind³ born here and her mama birthed her and gave her to the orphan house and left town. Her mama had a sister, but the sister had her own and didn't have time for no more mouths, she said. So the orphan home, a white one, had to keep her. They named her "Mary." Mary. Mary live there, well, "worked" there bout⁴ fifteen years, then they let

---

¹ever: every
²tention: attention
³mind: mine
⁴bout: about

her do outside work too and Mary saved her money and bought an acre of land just outside town for $5.00 and took to plantin it and growing things and when they were ready, she bring them into town and sell em. She made right smart⁵ a money too, cause soon as she could, she bought a little house over there at the end of the main street, long time ago, so it was cheap, and put up a little stall for her vegetables and added chickens and eggs and all fresh stuff, you know. Wasn't long fore⁶ she had a little store and added more things.

Now the mens took to hanging round her and things like that! She was a regular size woman, she had real short hair and little skinny bow legs, things like that, but she was real, real nice and a kind person . . . to everybody.

Anyway, pretty soon, one of them men with a mouth full of sugar and warm hands got to Mary. I always thought he had a mouth full of "gimme" and a hand full of "reach,"⁷ but when I tried to tell her, she just said, with her sweet soft smile, "maybe you just don't know him, he alright." Anyway, they got married.

Now he worked at Mr. Charlie's⁸ bar as a go-for and a clean-up man. After they got married I thought he would be working with Mary, in the field and in the store, you know. But he said he wasn't no field man and that that store work was woman's work lessen⁹ he stand at the cash register. But you know the business

---

⁵right smart: a lot
⁶fore: before
⁷mouth full of "gimme" and a hand full of "reach": selfish drive to have things his own way
⁸Mr Charlie's: *Mr. Charlie* is African-American slang for *white man*
⁹lessen: unless

wasn't that fast so wasn't nobody gonna be standing up in one spot all day doing nothing over that cigar box Mary used for a cash register.

Anyway, Mary must have loved him cause she liked to buy him things, things I knew that man never had; nice suits and shirts and shoes, socks and things like that. I was there once when she was so excited with a suit to give him and he just looked at it and flipped its edges and told her to "hang it up and I'll get to it when I can," said, "I wouldn'ta picked that one, but you can't help it if you got no eye for good things!" Can you magine!?[10] That man hadn't had nothing!! I could see he was changing, done spit that sugar out!![11]

Well, Mary's business picked up more and more and everybody came to get her fresh foods. It was a clean little store and soon she had a cash register and counters and soda water and canned goods and oh, all kinds of stuff you see in the big stores. She fixed that house up, too, and doing alright!! But, she didn't smile so much anymore . . . always looking thoughtful and a little in pain inside her heart. I took to helping her round the store and I began to see why she had changed. HE had changed! Charles, her husband! He was like hell on wheels with a automatic transmission! She couldn't do nothing right! She was dumb! Called her store a hole in the wall! Called her house "junk!" Said wasn't none of that stuff "nothing."

But I notice with the prosperity he quit working for Mr. Charlie and got a car and rode around and walked around and played around! Just doing nothing! And when people go to telling Mary how smart she was and how good she doing and they glad she there, I heard him say at least a hundred times, "I could take

---

[10]magine: imagine
[11]done spit that sugar out: no longer talked so sweetly

$100 and nothing and have more than this in a year!!"
Didn't like to see her happy and smiling! I think he
was jealous, but he coulda been working right beside
her! When he married her it was his business, too! I
heard her tell him that and guess what he answered? "I
don't need that hole in the wall with stuff sitting there
drawing flies, I'll think of something of my own!"
Lord, it's so many kinds of fools in the world you just
can't keep up with them!!

I went home to lunch with Mary once and he got
mad cause we woke him up as we was talking softly
and eating. Lord, did he talk about Mary! Talked about
her skinny legs and all under her clothes and her
kinky hair. She tried to keep it up but she worked and
sweat too hard, for him! She just dropped her head
deeper down into her plate and I could see she had a
hard time swallowing her food.

Then, she try to buy him something nice and he
told her to give it to the Salvation Army cause he didn't
want it and that he was going to give everything he
had to the Salvation Army that she had picked cause it
ain't what he liked! Ain't he something! Somebody
trying to be good to you and you ain't got sense
enough to understand kindness and love.

She cook good food for him, too, and he mess
with it and throw it out saying he don't like her cooking, he feel like eating out! Now!

Just let me tell you! She want a baby. He say he
don't want no nappy[12] head, skinny, bow-leg baby and
laughed at her.

She want to go out somewhere of a evening, he
say he ain't going nowhere with the grocery bag
woman!

---

[12]nappy: kinky-haired

I didn't mean to, but once I heard her ask him why he slept in the other bedroom stead[13] of with her one night—she had three bedrooms—and he said he couldn't help it, sometime he rather sleep with a rock, a big boulder, than her. She came back in with tears in her eyes that day, but she never complain, not to me anyway and I was her best friend.

Anyway, Mary took to eatin to get fat on her legs and bout five or six months, she was fat! Bout 200 pounds but her legs was still small and skinny and bowed. He really went to talking bout her then, even in the store, front of other people. Called her the Hog! Said everybody else's Hog[14] was a Cadillac but his was his wife! And laugh! He all the time laughing at her. They never laugh together, in front of me, anyway.

So, one day Mary say she going to take care some business for a few days and she went off alone. He say "Go head,[15] do what she want to do." He don't care bout what she do! "Do whatever!" Just like that! Whatever! Whatever! Didn't finish it like other people do, like "Whatever you want to," just, "Whatever!" I guess he heard it somewhere and thought it was smart to say it like that. Well, when Mary come back, I coulda fell out cause she brought one of her cousins, who was a real looker; long hair, big busts, and big legs and heart full of foolishness. Maybelline was her name and she worked in the store all day, I can't lie about that, she sure did help Mary, but where she got the strength, I don't know, cause she worked the men all night! In three or four months she had gone through all the legible[16] men in town, some twice, and then all the

---

[13]stead: instead
[14]Hog: *Hog* is a nickname for a Cadillac
[15]head: ahead
[16]legible: eligible, single

married illegible ones, some of them twice too. She was a go-getter, that Maybelline. But, she did help Mary and Mary seemed to need more help cause she was doing poorly in her health. She was sighing, tired and achy all the time now.

But she still took care of her business, the paper work and all, you know. Once, I saw Charles come into the store and she needed him to sign a few things, if you please, and he took them papers and bragged to the fellas in the store that "See, I got to sign things around here to keep things goin." He didn't even read them, just waved his hand and signed them and handed them to Mary without even looking at her, like she was a secretary or something, and went on out and drove off with a big grin looking 50¢ worth of importance, to me anyway.

Well, Mary just kep[17] getting worse off. I told her to see a doctor and she said she had in the big city and she had something they couldn't cure but she wish I wouldn't tell nobody, so I didn't. But I felt so bad for her I loved her. I knew whatever was killing her was started by a heavy sad heart, shaking hands, a sore spirit, hot tears, deep, heavy sighs, hurtful swallows and oh, you know, all them kinda things.

Soon she had to stay home in bed. Wasn't no long sickness though, I could see she was going fast. Near the end, one day I saw her out in her back yard picking up rocks and I knew the dear soul must be losing her mind also and I took her back in the house and tried to get her to let loose the rocks and throw them away, but she wouldn't let go. She was sick but she was strong in her hands, from all that work, I guess, she just held on to them, so I said, "Shit, you ain't never

---

[17]kep: kept

had too much you wanted to hold on to so hold the rocks if that what you want!" And she did.

Now, she asked Charles to take Maybelline back to the city to get the rest of Maybelline's things to move down there and Charles didn't mind at all cause I had seen him looking that Maybelline upways, downways, and both sideways and I could tell he liked what he saw and so could Maybelline cause she was always posing or prancing. Anyway, they went for a day, one night and back the next day. Before they went, I saw Charles sit on the side of Mary's bed and, first time I ever saw him do it, take her hand and hold it, then bend down and kiss her on the forehead. Musta been thinking bout what he was going to do to Maybelline while they was gone, but anyway, I'm glad he did do it. It brought tears to Mary's eyes. Then, they were gone and before they got back, Mary was gone.

I have to stop a minute cause everytime I think of that sweet woman. . . .

She had told me what to do, the funeral and all, so I had taken care of some of those things and Mary was already gone to the funeral home and the funeral was the next day.

When they come home or back, whatever!, all they had to do was get ready to go to the parlor.[18] I don't know when or nothing like that, but when Charles went to the closet to get something to wear, the closet was bare, except for a note: "Dear Charles," it say, "They gone to the Salvation Army just like you always say you want. Yours truly, Mary."

Now that man run all over trying to find some way to get them back but they was nice things and somebody had done bought them or either kept them, you know what I mean? Then, he rush over to the bank to get some money and found out his name

---

[18]parlor: funeral home

wasn't on the account no more! The manager gave him a letter say: "Dear Charles, You told me so many times you don't need me or nothing that is mine. Not going to force you to do nothing you don't want to do! Always, Mary."

His named was replaced with Maybelline's so naturally he went to see her at the store. She say sure, and give him $50 and he say, "Come go with me and help me pick it out," and she say she ain't got time. So he told her take time. She say, "I got to take care this business and close the store for the funeral." He say, "I'll close the store, this ain't your business to worry about." She say, "This my store." He say, "Are you crazy?" She say, "I ain't crazy. I'm the boss!" He say, "I'm Mary's husband, what's hers is mine!" She say, "That's true, but this store ain't hers, it's mine! I bought it from her!" He say, "With what? You can't afford to buy no store as nice as this!" She say, "Mary lent me the money; it's all legal; lawyer and everything!" He say, "How you gon'[19] pay her back? You got to pay me, bitch!" She say, "No . . . no . . . when Mary died, all debt clear." He say, "I'll see about that!" She say, "Here, here the lawyer's name and number." He snatched it and left. He musta found out she was right and it was legal cause I never heard no more about it.

Now everybody bringing food and all, the house was full, but I was among the last to go and when Charles got ready to go to bed he say he wasn't going to sleep in the room Mary died in and he went into the third bedroom. I heard him holler and went in there and the covers was pulled back and the bed was full of rocks . . . and a note say: "Dear Charles, Tried to get what you wanted, couldn't carry no boulder, honest. Yours, Mary." Me, I just left.

---

[19]gon': going to

Next morning he opens the food cupboard and it was almost empty, but for a note and note say: "Dear Charles, here is 30 days supply of food. Waste that too. Yours, Mary." I'm telling you, his life was going upside down. He and Maybelline stayed in that house alone together and that old Charles musta had something going on that was alright cause pretty soon they were married. I knew he thought he was marrying that store again, but let me tell you, Maybelline was pretty and fleshy but she couldn't count and didn't like to pay bills or the workers on that little piece of land of Mary's and pretty soon she was broke and the store was closed cause nothing wasn't in there but some old brown dead lettuce and turned up carrots and empty soda bottles and tired squashy tomatoes didn't nobody want. Charles didn't have nothing but an almost empty house. They cussed and fought and she finally left saying she wasn't really his wife cause she didn't have no divorce from her last husbands! So there!

Now, that ought to be all but let me finish telling you this cause I got to go now and see bout my own life.

Exactly a year passed from the day Mary had passed and a white lady and a black lady came to Mary's house with some papers and I heard a lot of hollering and shouting after a bit and Charles was putting them out. They waved those papers and said they would be back . . . and they did, a week later, with the Sheriff. Seems like Mary had give Charles one year to live there in the house and then it was to go, all legally, to be a orphan home for black children.

Welllll, when everything was over, I saw him sitting outside in his car, kinda raggedy now, just sitting there looking at the house. I took a deep breath and went to my dresser and got out the envelope Mary had give me to give him one year from her death, at this time. I looked at it awhile thinking bout all that had happened and feeling kind of sorry for Charles till I remembered we hoe our own rows and what we plants there, we picks.[20] So I went on out and handed him the envelope through the car window. He rolled me red eyes and a dirty look and opened the envelope and saw a one hundred dollar bill and . . . a note. He read it with a sad, sad look on his face. "Dear Charles, here is $100. Take all the nothing you want and in a year you'll have everything. Yours truly, your dead wife, Mary." Well, he just sat there a minute, staring at the money and the note, then started his car up and slowly drove away without so much as "good-by." Going somewhere to spend that money I guess, or just stop and stare off into space . . . Whatever!

REFLECT ······························

Where does Mary get the money to buy a house and open a store? What does this tell you about her?

In your opinion, why did Mary marry Charles? Why did he marry her? Why did she continue to live with Charles even though he treated her so badly?

Why did Mary bring Maybelline home with her? Do you think Mary imagined Charles and Maybelline would get together? Did Mary look ahead and foresee how that relationship would turn out?

Why did the writer choose to tell the story through Mary's friend rather than Mary herself?

---

[20]we hoe . . . and what we plants there, we picks: we are responsible for our own actions, and what we give, we get

WRITE ·

Mary worked hard to build a successful business. Write about a time when you worked hard to achieve a goal. What was the goal? Did you achieve everything you set out to? How did you feel?

Imagine that you are Mary's friend, and write a "Dear Abby" letter. Tell the advice columnist about your friend's problems, and ask her what you should do to help. Then imagine that you're Abby, and write back, giving your advice.

Reread the last paragraph of the story. Do you think Charles has learned anything from his experience? Describe what you imagine he is thinking as he drives slowly away. What do you think will happen to him now?

*Twice nominated for a National Book
Award, Robert Hayden (1913–1980) had
a very distinguished career as a poet.*

*How do parents express love for their chil-
dren? As you read, notice the ways in
which the father shows love for his son.*

Those Winter Sundays

Robert Hayden

Sundays too my father got up early
and put his clothes on in the blueblack cold,
then with cracked hands that ached
from labor in the weekday weather made
banked fires[1] blaze. No one ever thanked him.

I'd wake and hear the cold splintering, breaking.
When the rooms were warm, he'd call,
and slowly I would rise and dress,
fearing the chronic angers of that house,

Speaking indifferently to him,
who had driven out the cold
and polished my good shoes as well.
What did I know, what did I know
of love's austere[2] and lonely offices?[3]

---

[1]banked fires: fires built to burn slowly and evenly
[2]austere: stern
[3]offices: rituals

REFLECT ·

The son says that no one ever thanked his father for getting up early and warming the house. Do you think the father expected to be thanked?

The first line of the poem says, "Sundays too my father got up early." What does the word *too* tell you about the father's habits? What other clues in the poem tell you about his life? Describe it.

Why does the son speak "indifferently" to his father? How do you think the father feels when the son speaks to him that way?

What does the son mean when he speaks of "fearing the chronic angers of that house"? Who do you think was angry? At what?

How old do you think the son was when the action of the poem took place? How old do you think he is now? Have his feelings for his father changed? How can you tell?

WRITE ·

Family members often do things to help one another. Describe some small act of love that you regularly do or that someone does for you.

"Actions speak louder than words." Would the father agree with this old saying? Would the son? Explain what you think the father and son would say.

Looking back, the son says, "What did I know, what did I know." Imagine that you are he, and write a letter to the father. Tell him what you know now and how you learned it.

Fairfield Porter, *Seated Boy*, 1938, oil on masonite
The Parrish Art Museum, Southampton, New York
Photograph: Noel Rowe

When parents separate, who suffers more—the adults or the children? As you read, try to understand how each family member feels about the breakup.

Separating

Bo Caldwell

My mom is standing in the rain talking to the guy whose pickup she just rear-ended.[1] It's getting dark. We've pulled off the road and the two of them are under a tree next to his truck. He's younger than Mom, wearing jeans, a T-shirt, and cowboy boots. When they laugh, Mom looks like she does with her dates, these guys that shake my hand and call me Sport. It's Michael, I tell them, but they don't listen to a fourteen-year-old. He gets a notebook and pen from his truck, and they write things down and exchange pieces of paper while I wait in the car. I wait a lot lately, for school to end, or Mom to get home, or Dad to pick me up. They separated four months ago. Mostly I'm waiting for them to work things out.

Mom gets in the car and slams her door, which doesn't close quite like it did twenty minutes ago. She looks at her skirt. "I'm soaked," she says, as though it's a surprise, and she pushes her hair off her face. "He's nice. Lee, that's his name. He says we don't have to tell our insurance." This is big news. Mom's been to traffic school[2] twice.

"What's the catch?" I say, but she's not listening. She's watching the truck.

---

[1] rear-ended: struck from behind with her car
[2] traffic school: police-run safe-driving classes

"He's coming over later to give me the names of some body shops. I told him to come for dinner," she says, and she looks at me and shrugs.

It took Mom awhile to start dating. Dad used to ask me every week, first thing, Is she seeing anybody? And every week I'd shake my head, and Dad would seem half disappointed, half relieved. Until three weeks ago when she went out with Jim, a new teacher at the school where she's a speech therapist, and since then she's been a regular little social butterfly.[3] Dad took it like bad news he'd been expecting.

Dad, on the other hand, has done his fair share. Her name's Darilyn, and she's had pizza with us a few times. She drinks white wine with an ice cube, and never takes her sunglasses off. I stare at her nose when we talk; looking at her body feels weird, knowing what she and Dad are up to, and if I look at her eyes all I see is myself in the reflection of her glasses. I know that nose pretty well. The first time I met her, she and Dad acted like seeing each other was a big coincidence;[4] Dad was shy and excited around her, then on the way home he asked me in a confidential,[5] buddy-buddy tone to please not mention her to Mom. I don't want to hurt her any more than I have, he said. Is she why you moved out, I said, but he wouldn't answer.

Dad called us every day the first few weeks he was gone; sometimes Mom would talk to him, sometimes not. She acted as though he were just on a trip, and got mad if I asked when he was coming home. Then we saw him at the market. He'd seen Mom's car on Lake Street, he said, and he'd followed us. He

---

[3]social butterfly: person who has an active social life
[4]coincidence: accidental occurrence
[5]confidential: secretive

walked with us through the aisles, saying he was sorry things were like this, asking how we were, was there anything he could do. Would you be quiet, Mom said, we're in the market, as she squeezed our cart past Mrs. Markey, the school counselor, who gave Mom a look. You've flipped,[6] Mom whispered to Dad. If you think I'm just going to sit around until your little crisis is over, you're crazier than I thought. She put some bananas in our cart, weighed a bag of oranges, while Dad and I looked on. Jean, he said, I'm forty-six years old and I felt ten years older than that with you. I felt like things were closing in on me in that house, and he waved his arm as though he meant the market, the town. Us. Mom was tying a knot in the bag of oranges, pulling hard at the corners. What did you expect, that's what I'd like to know, she said, from people like us with a son? You didn't turn out to be the person I thought you were, Dad said, looking away from her. You mean she's not Darilyn, I wanted to say, but I kept quiet. Mom started pushing the cart fast, almost running from him. This is a goddamn market, she said, louder than she meant to. People stared, a cashier stopped ringing things up and looked our way. Mom turned down the cereal aisle, barely missing a box boy putting jars of peanut butter on a shelf, where she abandoned[7] our cart and headed for the exit. Come on, Michael, she said, let's get out of here. Dad tried to take her arm, but she shook him off. Go to hell, Grady, she said, and when he stared at her with his hangdog[8] look, she said, Look, what did you expect? You weren't exactly trying to win some popularity contest, were you? Her words seemed to ring out in the store. I

---

[6]flipped: lost your mind
[7]abandoned: left
[8]hangdog: sad

looked at the linoleum floor and kicked at a piece of lettuce as we walked out, wishing we were invisible.

Little things have changed since then. We eat out a lot; Mom says it's a lot of trouble to cook for two. She has the radio on, all the time, news, sports, easy listening, she doesn't care what, as long as it's noise. And the house. Every day Mom puts a few more of Dad's things in the den: books, albums, his tools from the garage, quilts passed down from his mom, his clothes. I hear her late at night, sorting things, moving things, and if I come out of my room she stops, wide-eyed, as though I've caught her at something furtive,[9] then she goes back to what she was doing without saying anything. It sounds like there are rats in our house.

Mom and I drive to Monty's, where Dad's picking me up tonight. Mom doesn't like him coming to the house—she says it makes it hard to keep her distance—so we meet at different places around town, where we try to act like nothing's wrong. Mom likes to get us there early enough to sit down and have something to drink while we wait for Dad. It's always awkward; I think she's trying to be nice to me.

Monty's has dim lights, dark-red vinyl booths, and paper placemats with maps that have gold stars to show where the other Monty's are. Mom and I sit in a corner booth and she orders our usual: a glass of wine for her, a Coke with lime for me. The lime is her idea; she says it's festive.[10]

"Well, we made it to another Friday night," she says. "Cheers," and she clinks my glass. "This must be hard for you. When I was fourteen everything was so set. No ifs, you know?"

"It's all right," I say.

---

[9]furtive: secret
[10]festive: suitable for a party

"I wasn't apologizing, Michael." She hands me my napkin, the heavy cloth kind, the same dark red as the booths.

"I didn't say you were."

She straightens her silverware, then looks around like she's trying to find someone she knows. "I didn't think I'd end up like this. A single mom, a place like this on a Friday night."

"The baseball team had their awards banquet here last year," I say. That's the trick with Mom: keep the conversation light, don't let her start considering things.

Mom smooths her placemat where her glass has made it wet. "I think we're doing better. I feel like I'm coming out of this. Maybe it isn't the worst thing that could have happened, you know?"

"You're doing great," I say, my voice high and fake, and I wish again that they wouldn't talk to me about their marriage, or their divorce, whatever it is they have. "I wish it were a year from now," I say.

Mom nods. "I'm not too crazy about the near future either." She sighs. "Who knows? Maybe this is just wife talk, mumbo-jumbo[11] talk. Maybe I just gave you a great big earful of wife talk is all, do you think?" She rubs my cheek and smiles. I started shaving a few weeks ago, just before school started. "You're so big," she says. "We never expected that."

We stare at the table. I squeeze some lime into my Coke, drop the rind into it, and stir it around. I'm getting used to the taste of lime. I try to think about predictable things like geometry, soccer, that great smell of some girls' hair. Then I see Mom look up and sigh, a noise like our house makes in the night, settling, and I know that Dad's here. Mom smooths her hair.

---

[11]mumbo-jumbo: meaningless

Dad leans down and kisses Mom's cheek, something he used to do every night when he came home from work, but there's an apology in it tonight, and it feels like a small conversation's taken place between them.

"I didn't see you," he says.

Mom nods. "It's dark. I knew there was a reason we never ate here." She won't go to our old places.

Dad's hair is wet from the rain. He seems nervous and excited, and it occurs to me that maybe he has Darilyn stashed[12] in the car. "Your front bumper looks funny," he says, as he stares at the table and moves the salt closer to the pepper.

"I know. I'll pay for it," Mom says.

"I wasn't worried about the money," he says. "You always think I'm going to say something bad."

"Since when do you know what I think?" she says. Dad looks at the ceiling, which sparkles. Mom picks up the check, puts some money on the table, and stands. She smooths her skirt, which is still damp, and Dad and I follow her out.

Dad drives to the pizza place where we go every week. I sit at our same table, the one in the back under the neon Miller sign, while Dad gets a pitcher of beer and a Coke.

"Drink your Coke," he says when he sits down.

"I'm not thirsty."

"Trust me," he says. "Just drink it." He watches me while I down it, then he takes my empty glass, looks around the room, and fills it with beer. This is the second time he's given me beer. The first time was on our second night out when I cried. I don't know why I did that, except that it all hit me at once: Mom's

---

[12]stashed: hidden away

weirdness, Dad's scatteredness, how screwed up everything was. Dad said stupid things about the passage of time, which he knew as well as I did was bull, so he finally just shut up and gave me a beer.

"We're celebrating," Dad says as he puts my glass down in front of me. He clinks it with his mug. "To reunions."

I watch him drink. He puts his mug down and leans forward, anxious, waiting. "Well, what do you think?" he says. "About your mom and me."

I put my glass down a little too loudly, and the waiter glances at us. "You mean like you're getting back together?"

"The very thing," Dad says. "As of tonight." He lowers his voice. "I made a mistake. But it's over now."

"When did you tell Mom?"

"We're telling her tonight. You and me. There's a bottle of Emerald Dry[13] in the trunk. I figured after dinner we'd go home and celebrate. The three of us." I can feel him staring at me, and when I don't say anything he roughs up my hair. "Hey, who died? We're talking good news here."

"What happened to Darilyn?"

He shrugs, looks away. "She went back," he says. "Back?"

"To her husband, all right?" He glares at me.

"Okay." We're quiet for a minute. I hate this place. Dad thinks it's a real find. "Maybe you should talk to Mom alone," I say.

"I want to surprise her."

"She'll be surprised," I say, and I finish my beer and wait for him to fill my glass.

When I was ten, Mom was in an accident, not her first or last, just another one. It was raining, and she'd

---

[13]Emerald Dry: brand of wine

slammed on the brakes to avoid the guy in front of her who'd stopped unexpectedly, and she'd spun out in the middle of the expressway before sliding off the road onto a soft shoulder. Dad and I were following her at the time; we were supposed to be taking her car in for service. Dad managed a garage and used to do all the work on her car himself, before he got too busy. I was in the front seat with him, and it was the panic on his face, not the sight of Mom's car facing us like bumper cars,[14] that scared me. We pulled off the road, and Dad made me lie down on the seat before he got out. Don't get up till I say, he'd told me, then he'd slammed the door and run to her car. I did look, though. Mom got out shaking her head, pushing her hair off her face, and I strained to see if she was hurt. But she was fine. She smiled, looked embarrassed. Dad held her tightly and I could see her struggling to pull away from him. Would you stop worrying about me? she said. Dad turned and walked to the car. I put my head down on the seat until he opened his door and told me in a tight voice that everything was okay.

Dad pulls into our driveway and stops the car. "Home sweet home," he says, and he smiles at me. He gets out and opens the trunk. "Voila!"[15] He holds up a bottle of wine. "Our old standby."[16] He closes the trunk and starts up the walk, then turns to me. "Come on, bud."

"Dad," I say, "I think we should have called. We're pretty early."

---

[14]bumper cars: padded cars on a carnival ride in which people intentionally drive into each other
[15]Voila!: Here it is!
[16]standby: favorite

"It's okay," he says, then he stops, listening. We can hear music, the Righteous Brothers[17] album Mom plays when she's in a good mood. Dad marches up the steps, pushes his hair off his forehead, knocks.

"Dad," I whisper, but he waves me away, so I just stand behind him, feeling panicked, wanting him to do something the way when I was five and I swallowed a Reed's cinnamon drop he picked me up by my ankles and shook me until it popped out of my mouth. Part of me wants him to walk into this. Let him see how it feels, making a fool of himself, the way I feel on our little rendezvous[18] with Darilyn.

We hear footsteps, the click click click of high heels, Mom calling, "It's about time!" Then she opens the door. "Oh," she says, when she sees us, and she looks at her watch.

I can't tell who's more surprised. Dad stares at her with his mouth open. She's wearing the dark-blue dress she wears when she and Dad go out, and her night perfume. She's holding the blender, which is full of something pale and icy.

"Well," she says. "Come on in, I guess."

Dad glances at me then steps inside.

"What's that for?" Mom says, staring at the wine.

Dad looks at it as though he's surprised to see it. "I don't know," he says in a flat voice. He hands it to her. "What are you making?"

"Margaritas." She puts the wine and the blender on the table where we keep the mail.

"It's getting cold," Dad says suddenly, and he glances behind him as though right this minute fall is setting in. "I need a sweater. I didn't take any with me. It was summer."

---

[17]Righteous Brothers: popular romantic singers
[18]rendezvous: secret meeting

Mom closes the door. "Have a seat. I've got them in a box," and she starts down the hall, her heels clicking again.

"In a box," Dad says, staring after her. He looks at me. "She's got them in a box."

"All your stuff's in boxes," Mom calls cheerfully from the den. "You can wait in the living room."

"We can wait," he says, and I follow him into our living room, which smells like furniture polish. There are roses on the table. I feel like a guest, like I should have put on clean clothes and wiped my feet before I came in.

Dad looks at me suddenly. "Who's she seeing tonight?" he whispers.

I shrug. "The guy she hit today. He's supposed to come for dinner."

"Nice of you to let me know," he says.

I start to say something back to him, but Mom walks in carrying a cardboard box that says "Sweaters" in thick black Marks-a-lot.[19]

Dad sits in his chair, the one Mom always wants to throw out because it's so worn. "You expecting someone?" he says.

Mom blushes. "It was sort of up in the air."

"Who?" he says. She ignores him. He sniffs. "What are you cooking?"

"Shish kebab."

Dad looks at me. "Wouldn't you know it," he says. "Shish kebab. I hate shish kebab."

"I don't see what my dinner menu has to do with you," Mom says.

Dad stands and walks around the room. "I like this room," he says.

---

[19]Marks-a-lot: brand of marking pen

Mom holds the box out to him. "Here, these are your sweaters," she says in her time-to-go voice, the one she uses when she's had enough of my friends.

Dad puts the box on the floor and pulls out a blue sweater with patches. I can smell mothballs. "This is the one I want," he says. "I remember when you gave it to me."

"You might as well take all of them," Mom says.

"I don't want all of them," Dad says. "I want this one." He looks at me. "Some celebration," he says.

Mom puts the lid back on the box. "Just what were you planning on celebrating, Grady?"

"Your date," Dad says, "your big date. That and my sweaters. You aren't wasting any time getting my stuff packed up." He looks around the room. There are spaces in the bookshelves from where Mom's taken Dad's books out; the paint on the walls is yellow in places where she's taken down pictures of him. The only thing of his in the room, besides the box of sweaters, is his chair, which she said was too heavy. She was going to call Goodwill[20] next week. "Where is everything?"

"In the den," Mom says. "You haven't exactly acted like all this was temporary. Getting your own place, coming by for clothes."

"This isn't what I wanted," he says. "You can't just decide—"

"Grady," she says, and I can see the gentleness in her voice is killing him. "Listen. What's happened is for the best. I didn't think that at first, but I do now. You were right to leave. I never would have done it, but you were right. We'll be better off."

---

[20]Goodwill: charitable group

Dad's standing near the wall where a picture of him fishing used to hang. "I hate better off," he says. He rubs the wall and turns to Mom. "You took the nails out."

"They're my nails," she says.

"The hell they are," he says. "If you think—"

"Would you shut up about the nails," I say. "Our house looks like we've been cleaned out and you're fighting about nails. Why do you have to fight so much?"

"You don't understand, Michael," Dad says quietly.

"Oh, really? I understand that the den looks like Bekins[21] is about to pull up for your stuff. I understand that I hate being at home now. That I dread being in the same room with my parents." Dad and I stare at each other. "Tell Mom your big news." He doesn't move. "Come on, tell her about your plans."

"I don't have any plans," he says flatly.

"Tell Mom about how Darilyn drinks wine with an ice cube in it, about her shades. About how she's gone back to her husband."

Mom is standing at the window, looking out, her back to us. She turns, faces me. "I don't need to hear this from you," she says.

"Fine. Don't. Listen to him, the all-time answer man," and I head for the door. They don't say anything as I slam it behind me.

I hear Mom calling me, Michael, Michael? all the way up the block, but I don't turn around. Finally she stops, and I walk back to our house and sit on the curb across the street. Dad comes out after a while and drives away without seeing me.

---

[21]Bekins: large moving company

Mom goes out the side door and I go up the driveway to her. She's been crying.

"Can I hold you?" she says when she sees me, and I nod. She puts her arms around me. It's awkward. I'm taller than she is, and I don't know what to do with my hands.

"I get my strength from you," she says. "When you were little, and we'd fight, I used to come in and hold you while you were sleeping." She lets go of me and puts her hand on my arm. "You felt so sturdy, so strong."

"I don't feel strong. I feel like things are falling apart."

"They are. But you'll be okay." She looks pretty in this light. It makes me think of the times she and Dad would go out, her all dressed up, him with his arm around her waist.

"I'm sorry," I start, but she shakes her head.

"It's okay. We've done a pretty good job of messing up our lives, I guess." She wipes her eyes, then looks at me as though she hasn't seen me for a long time. "You're really starting to look like him. Maybe that's not all bad." She kisses my cheek and goes inside.

I sit down on the steps. It's cold. I can see my breath, but I don't go in. The people across the street are eating their dinner, laughing and passing plates. I wonder if they saw this coming, this divorce. I wonder if we show. We're afraid of hurting each other in my family, of being too rough, and I wish I could change us. But what I do is watch those people across the street, watch them until they've left the table, until the mother has cleared the dishes and turned out the light.

REFLECT ································

Whose choice was it that Michael's parents should separate? What were the reasons for the separation?

How did Michael's mother feel about her husband during the first weeks of their separation? Have her feelings changed? How can you tell?

What reason does Michael's father give for wanting to return home? Do you think this reason is the only one? Why or why not?

Children often get caught in the middle when their parents don't get along. In your opinion, is this happening to Michael? Explain.

WRITE ·······························

Do you think that a man and woman no longer in love should stay together for the sake of their children? Explain.

Imagine that the father in the story has asked you for advice. He wonders whether he should try to win back his wife or give up on the relationship. What would you tell him? Why?

Will Michael's parents get back together? Explain what you think will happen to them.

*In many families, it is a tradition to make
wishes before blowing out the candles on
a birthday cake. When you were a child,
what kinds of things did you wish for?
Have the things you wish for changed as
you have grown older? As you read, compare your wishes with the speaker's. Ask
yourself what exactly it is that she wishes
she could tell her husband.*

The Birthday

Philip Dacey

Thirty candles and one
to grow on. My husband
and son watch me
think of wishes.

I wish I found it
easier to make wishes
than I do. Wasn't it,
years ago, easy to make wishes?

My husband and son *are* wishes.
It is as if
every day I wait for them
to happen again,

and they do.
But surely there is much
I am without, yet
I stand here, wishless.

Perhaps I want
what I needn't wish for,
my life: it is
coming, everything will happen.

Or perhaps I want
precisely what I don't know,
all that darkness
so tall and handsome before me.

I have seen women age
beautifully, with a
growing, luminous[1]
sexuality:

now I know, each year
they've been slowly
stepping out of their wishes
like their clothes.

I stand here amazed
at what is happening to me,
how I've begun to lighten
of desires, getting down

to my secret skin,
the impossibly thin
membrane[2] this side
of nothing. Husband,

I wish I could tell you.

---

[1]luminous: glowing
[2]membrane: flexible covering

REFLECT ·····································

How old is the woman in the poem? Why is this birthday often considered to be a special one?

Why does the woman find it hard to make wishes? Does she believe this difficulty is harmful?

Is the woman satisfied with how her life has turned out so far? How can you tell?

How would you define the difference between aging and maturing?

In your opinion, is the poem about growing older? Growing wiser? Both?

WRITE ·································

What is your greatest wish for yourself? For your family? For the world? Make a wish list.

Some families develop their own traditions for celebrating birthdays or other special occasions, such as holidays. Choose a special occasion, and describe how your family celebrates it.

Many folk stories and jokes are about someone who gets what he or she wants and then regrets it. Write about a time when you got what you wanted and later were sorry you did.

Henri Matisse, *Femme Assise devant Son Piano*, 1924,
   oil on canvas
from the Sotheby's sale of June 23, 1965, Lot 75
Copyright 1994 Succession H. Matisse/ARS, New York

Award-winning author Amy Tan is best known for her novels. The story below is from The Joy Luck Club, *her first novel. You might enjoy watching the movie version of this popular book.*

As a child, did you ever do something because your parents wanted you to? Perhaps you took music lessons or played a sport or joined an organization. In this story, a mother forces her daughter to take piano lessons. As you read, ask yourself, Why is the mother so determined to find a special talent in her daughter? Why is the daughter so determined not to develop it?

Two Kinds

From *The Joy Luck Club*

Amy Tan

My mother believed you could be anything you wanted to be in America. You could open a restaurant. You could work for the government and get good retirement. You could buy a house with almost no money down. You could become rich. You could become instantly famous.

"Of course you can be prodigy,[1] too," my mother told me when I was nine. "You can be best anything. What does Auntie Lindo know? Her daughter, she is only best tricky."

America was where all my mother's hopes lay. She had come here in 1949 after losing everything in

---

[1]prodigy: extraordinarily talented person

China: her mother and father, her family home, her first husband, and two daughters, twin baby girls. But she never looked back with regret. There were so many ways for things to get better.

We didn't immediately pick the right kind of prodigy. At first my mother thought I could be a Chinese Shirley Temple.[2] We'd watch Shirley's old movies on TV as though they were training films. My mother would poke my arm and say, "*Ni kan*"—You watch. And I would see Shirley tapping her feet, or singing a sailor song, or pursing her lips into a very round O while saying, "Oh my goodness."

"*Ni kan*," said my mother as Shirley's eyes flooded with tears. "You already know how. Don't need talent for crying!"

Soon after my mother got this idea about Shirley Temple, she took me to a beauty training school in the Mission district[3] and put me in the hands of a student who could barely hold the scissors without shaking. Instead of getting big fat curls, I emerged with an uneven mass of crinkly black fuzz. My mother dragged me off to the bathroom and tried to wet down my hair.

"You look like Negro Chinese," she lamented, as if I had done this on purpose.

The instructor of the beauty training school had to lop off these soggy clumps to make my hair even again. "Peter Pan[4] is very popular these days," the instructor assured my mother. I now had hair the length of a boy's, with straight-across bangs that hung at a slant two inches above my eyebrows. I liked the haircut and it made me actually look forward to my future fame.

---

[2]Shirley Temple: curly-haired child star of the 1930s
[3]Mission district: section of San Francisco
[4]Peter Pan: childlike main character in the play of the same name

In fact, in the beginning, I was just as excited as my mother, maybe even more so. I pictured this prodigy part of me as many different images, trying each one on for size. I was a dainty ballerina girl standing by the curtains, waiting to hear the right music that would send me floating on my tiptoes. I was like the Christ child lifted out of the straw manger, crying with holy indignity. I was Cinderella stepping from her pumpkin carriage with sparkly cartoon music filling the air.

In all of my imaginings, I was filled with a sense that I would soon become *perfect.* My mother and father would adore me. I would be beyond reproach. I would never feel the need to sulk for anything.

But sometimes the prodigy in me became impatient. "If you don't hurry up and get me out of here, I'm disappearing for good," it warned. "And then you'll always be nothing."

Every night after dinner, my mother and I would sit at the Formica kitchen table. She would present new tests, taking her examples from stories of amazing children she had read in *Ripley's Believe It or Not,* or *Good Housekeeping, Reader's Digest,* and a dozen other magazines she kept in a pile in our bathroom. My mother got these magazines from people whose houses she cleaned. And since she cleaned many houses each week, we had a great assortment. She would look through them all, searching for stories about remarkable children.

The first night she brought out a story about a three-year-old boy who knew the capitals of all the states and even most of the European countries. A teacher was quoted as saying the little boy could also pronounce the names of the foreign cities correctly.

"What's the capital of Finland?" my mother asked me, looking at the magazine story.

All I knew was the capital of California, because Sacramento was the name of the street we lived on in Chinatown. "Nairobi!" I guessed, saying the most foreign word I could think of. She checked to see if that was possibly one way to pronounce "Helsinki" before showing me the answer.

The tests got harder—multiplying numbers in my head, finding the queen of hearts in a deck of cards, trying to stand on my head without using my hands, predicting the daily temperatures in Los Angeles, New York, and London.

One night I had to look at a page from the Bible for three minutes and then report everything I could remember. "Now Jehoshaphat had riches and honor in abundance and . . . that's all I remember, Ma," I said.

And after seeing my mother's disappointed face once again, something inside of me began to die. I hated the tests, the raised hopes and failed expectations. Before going to bed that night, I looked in the mirror above the bathroom sink and when I saw only my face staring back—and that it would always be this ordinary face—I began to cry. Such a sad, ugly girl! I made high-pitched noises like a crazed animal, trying to scratch out the face in the mirror.

And then I saw what seemed to be the prodigy side of me—because I had never seen that face before. I looked at my reflection, blinking so I could see more clearly. The girl staring back at me was angry, powerful. This girl and I were the same. I had new thoughts, willful thoughts, or rather thoughts filled with lots of won'ts. I won't let her change me, I promised myself. I won't be what I'm not.

So now on nights when my mother presented her tests, I performed listlessly,[5] my head propped on one

---

[5]listlessly: without interest or enthusiasm

arm. I pretended to be bored. And I was. I got so bored I started counting the bellows of the foghorns out on the bay while my mother drilled me in other areas. The sound was comforting and reminded me of the cow jumping over the moon. And the next day, I played a game with myself, seeing if my mother would give up on me before eight bellows. After a while I usually counted only one, maybe two bellows at most. At last she was beginning to give up hope.

Two or three months had gone by without any mention of my being a prodigy again. And then one day my mother was watching *The Ed Sullivan Show*[6] on TV. The TV was old and the sound kept shorting out. Every time my mother got halfway up from the sofa to adjust the set, the sound would go back on and Ed would be talking. As soon as she sat down, Ed would go silent again. She got up, the TV broke into loud piano music. She sat down. Silence. Up and down, back and forth, quiet and loud. It was like a stiff embraceless dance between her and the TV set. Finally she stood by the set with her hand on the sound dial.

She seemed entranced[7] by the music, a little frenzied[8] piano piece with this mesmerizing[9] quality, sort of quick passages and then teasing lilting ones before it returned to the quick playful parts.

"*Ni kan*," my mother said, calling me over with hurried hand gestures, "Look here."

I could see why my mother was fascinated by the music. It was being pounded out by a little Chinese girl, about nine years old, with a Peter Pan haircut. The

---

[6] *The Ed Sullivan Show*: popular 1950s and 1960s variety show
[7] entranced: under the spell of
[8] frenzied: wild
[9] mesmerizing: bewitching

girl had the sauciness[10] of a Shirley Temple. She was proudly modest like a proper Chinese child. And she also did this fancy sweep of a curtsy,[11] so that the fluffy skirt of her white dress cascaded[12] slowly to the floor like the petals of a large carnation.

In spite of these warning signs, I wasn't worried. Our family had no piano and we couldn't afford to buy one, let alone reams of sheet music and piano lessons. So I could be generous in my comments when my mother bad-mouthed the little girl on TV.

"Play note right, but doesn't sound good! No singing sound," complained my mother.

"What are you picking on her for?" I said carelessly. "She's pretty good. Maybe she's not the best, but she's trying hard." I knew almost immediately I would be sorry I said that.

"Just like you," she said. "Not the best. Because you not trying." She gave a little huff as she let go of the sound dial and sat down on the sofa.

The little Chinese girl sat down also to play an encore of "Anitra's Dance" by Grieg. I remember the song, because later on I had to learn how to play it.

Three days after watching *The Ed Sullivan Show*, my mother told me what my schedule would be for piano lessons and piano practice. She had talked to Mr. Chong, who lived on the first floor of our apartment building. Mr. Chong was a retired piano teacher and my mother had traded housecleaning services for weekly lessons and a piano for me to practice on every day, two hours a day, from four until six.

---

[10]sauciness: boldness
[11]curtsy: bow
[12]cascaded: flowed

When my mother told me this, I felt as though I had been sent to hell. I whined and then kicked my foot a little when I couldn't stand it anymore.

"Why don't you like me the way I am? I'm *not* a genius! I can't play the piano. And even if I could, I wouldn't go on TV if you paid me a million dollars!" I cried.

My mother slapped me. "Who ask you be genius?" she shouted. "Only ask you be your best. For you sake. You think I want you be genius? Hnnh! What for! Who ask you!"

"So ungrateful," I heard her mutter in Chinese. "If she had as much talent as she has temper, she would be famous now."

Mr. Chong, whom I secretly nicknamed Old Chong, was very strange, always tapping his fingers to the silent music of an invisible orchestra. He looked ancient in my eyes. He had lost most of the hair on top of his head and he wore thick glasses and had eyes that always looked tired and sleepy. But he must have been younger than I thought, since he lived with his mother and was not yet married.

I met Old Lady Chong once and that was enough. She had this peculiar smell like a baby that had done something in its pants. And her fingers felt like a dead person's, like an old peach I once found in the back o the refrigerator; the skin just slid off the meat when picked it up.

I soon found out why Old Chong had retired fr teaching piano. He was deaf. "Like Beethoven!"[13] shouted to me. "We're both listening only in head!" And he would start to conduct his frantic sonatas.[14]

---

[13]Beethoven: German composer (1770–1827) who deaf

[14]sonata: musical piece in several parts

Our lessons went like this. He would open the book and point to different things, explaining their purpose: "Key! Treble! Bass! No sharps or flats! So this is C major! Listen now and play after me!"

And then he would play the C scale a few times, a simple chord, and then, as if inspired by an old, unreachable itch, he gradually added more notes and running trills and a pounding bass until the music was really something quite grand.

I would play after him, the simple scale, the simple chord, and then I just played some nonsense that sounded like a cat running up and down on top of garbage cans. Old Chong smiled and applauded and then said, "Very good! But now you must learn to keep time!"

So that's how I discovered that Old Chong's eyes were too slow to keep up with the wrong notes I was playing. He went through the motions in half-time. To help me keep rhythm, he stood behind me, pushing down on my right shoulder for every beat. He balanced pennies on top of my wrists so I would keep them still as I slowly played scales and arpeggios.[15] He me curve my hand around an apple and keep that when playing chords. He marched stiffly to me how to make each finger dance up and staccato[16] like an obedient little soldier.

taught me all these things, and that was how I earned I could be lazy and get away with missing lots of mistakes. If I hit the wrong notes because just practiced enough, I never corrected myself. I dut playing in rhythm. And Old Chong kept coning his own private reverie.[17]

maybe I never really gave myself a fair chance.

---

[15]arpeg: notes of a chord played one by one
[16]staccatt hythmically
[17]reverie: eam

I did pick up the basics pretty quickly, and I might have become a good pianist at that young age. But I was so determined not to try, not to be anybody different that I learned to play only the most ear-splitting preludes,[18] the most discordant[19] hymns.

Over the next year, I practiced like this, dutifully in my own way. And then one day I heard my mother and her friend Lindo Jong both talking in a loud bragging tone of voice so others could hear. It was after church, and I was leaning against the brick wall wearing a dress with stiff white petticoats. Auntie Lindo's daughter, Waverly, who was about my age, was standing farther down the wall about five feet away. We had grown up together and shared all the closeness of two sisters squabbling[20] over crayons and dolls. In other words, for the most part, we hated each other. I thought she was snotty. Waverly Jong had gained a certain amount of fame as "Chinatown's Littlest Chinese Chess Champion."

"She bring home too many trophy," lamented Auntie Lindo that Sunday. "All day she play chess. All day I have no time do nothing but dust off her winnings." She threw a scolding look at Waverly, who pretended not to see her.

"You lucky you don't have this problem," said Auntie Lindo with a sigh to my mother.

And my mother squared her shoulders and bragged: "Our problem worser than yours. If we ask Jing-mei wash dish, she hear nothing but music. It's like you can't stop this natural talent."

And right then, I was determined to put a stop to her foolish pride.

---

[18]prelude: introductory part of a musical piece
[19]discordant: unharmonious, sour-sounding
[20]squabbling: arguing

A few weeks later, Old Chong and my mother conspired to have me play in a talent show which would be held in the church hall. By then, my parents had saved up enough to buy me a secondhand piano, a black Wurlitzer spinet with a scarred bench. It was the showpiece of our living room.

For the talent show, I was to play a piece called "Pleading Child" from Schumann's *Scenes from Childhood*. It was a simple, moody piece that sounded more difficult than it was. I was supposed to memorize the whole thing, playing the repeat parts twice to make the piece sound longer. But I dawdled over it, playing a few bars and then cheating, looking up to see what notes followed. I never really listened to what I was playing. I daydreamed about being somewhere else, about being someone else.

The part I liked to practice best was the fancy curtsy: right foot out, touch the rose on the carpet with a pointed foot, sweep to the side, left leg bends, look up and smile.

My parents invited all the couples from the Joy Luck Club[21] to witness my debut. Auntie Lindo and Uncle Tin were there. Waverly and her two older brothers had also come. The first two rows were filled with children both younger and older than I was. The littlest ones got to go first. They recited simple nursery rhymes, squawked out tunes on miniature violins, twirled Hula Hoops,[22] pranced in pink ballet tutus,[23] and when they bowed or curtsied, the audience would sigh in unison, "Awww," and then clap enthusiastically.

---

[21]Joy Luck Club: social group formed by Chinese immigrant families in the novel of the same name
[22]Hula Hoop: circular plastic tubing twirled around the waist; popular toy during the 1950s
[23]tutus: short, fluffy skirts

When my turn came, I was very confident. I remember my childish excitement. It was as if I knew, without a doubt, that the prodigy side of me really did exist. I had no fear whatsoever, no nervousness. I remember thinking to myself, This is it! This is it! I looked out over the audience, at my mother's blank face, my father's yawn, Auntie Lindo's stiff-lipped smile, Waverly's sulky expression. I had on a white dress layered with sheets of lace, and a pink bow in my Peter Pan haircut. As I sat down I envisioned[24] people jumping to their feet and Ed Sullivan rushing up to introduce me to everyone on TV.

And I started to play. It was so beautiful. I was so caught up in how lovely I looked that at first I didn't worry how I would sound. So it was a surprise to me when I hit the first wrong note and I realized something didn't sound quite right. And then I hit another and another followed that. A chill started at the top of my head and began to trickle down. Yet I couldn't stop playing, as though my hands were bewitched. I kept thinking my fingers would adjust themselves back, like a train switching to the right track. I played this strange jumble through two repeats, the sour notes staying with me all the way to the end.

When I stood up, I discovered my legs were shaking. Maybe I had just been nervous and the audience, like Old Chong, had seen me go through the right motions and had not heard anything wrong at all. I swept my right foot out, went down on my knee, looked up and smiled. The room was quiet, except for Old Chong, who was beaming and shouting, "Bravo! Bravo! Well done!" But then I saw my mother's face, her stricken[25] face. The audience clapped weakly, and as I walked back to my chair, with my whole face

---

[24]envisioned: pictured
[25]stricken: horrified

quivering as I tried not to cry, I heard a little boy whisper loudly to his mother, "That was awful," and the mother whispered back, "Well, she certainly tried."

And now I realized how many people were in the audience, the whole world it seemed. I was aware of eyes burning into my back. I felt the shame of my mother and father as they sat stiffly throughout the rest of the show.

We could have escaped during intermission. Pride and some strange sense of honor must have anchored my parents to their chairs. And so we watched it all: the eighteen-year-old boy with a fake mustache who did a magic show and juggled flaming hoops while riding a unicycle. The breasted girl with white makeup who sang from *Madama Butterfly* and got honorable mention. And the eleven-year-old boy who won first prize playing a tricky violin song that sounded like a busy bee.

After the show, the Hsus, the Jongs, and the St. Clairs from the Joy Luck Club came up to my mother and father.

"Lots of talented kids," Auntie Lindo said vaguely, smiling broadly.

"That was somethin' else," said my father, and I wondered if he was referring to me in a humorous way, or whether he even remembered what I had done.

Waverly looked at me and shrugged her shoulders. "You aren't a genius like me," she said matter-of-factly. And if I hadn't felt so bad, I would have pulled her braids and punched her stomach.

But my mother's expression was what devastated[26] me: a quiet, blank look that said she had lost everything. I felt the same way, and

---

[26]devastated: destroyed

it seemed as if everybody were now coming up, like gawkers at the scene of an accident, to see what parts were actually missing. When we got on the bus to go home, my father was humming the busy-bee tune and my mother was silent. I kept thinking she wanted to wait until we got home before shouting at me. But when my father unlocked the door to our apartment, my mother walked in and then went to the back, into the bedroom. No accusations. No blame. And in a way, I felt disappointed. I had been waiting for her to start shouting, so I could shout back and cry and blame her for all my misery.

I assumed my talent-show fiasco[27] meant I never had to play the piano again. But two days later, after school, my mother came out of the kitchen and saw me watching TV.

"Four clock," she reminded me as if it were any other day. I was stunned, as though she were asking me to go through the talent-show torture again. I wedged myself more tightly in front of the TV.

"Turn off TV," she called from the kitchen five minutes later.

I didn't budge. And then I decided. I didn't have to do what my mother said anymore. I wasn't her slave. This wasn't China. I had listened to her before and look what happened. She was the stupid one.

She came out from the kitchen and stood in the arched entryway of the living room. "Four clock," she said once again, louder.

"I'm not going to play anymore," I said nonchalantly.[28] "Why should I? I'm not a genius."

---

[27]fiasco: disaster
[28]nonchalantly: coolly

She walked over and stood in front of the TV. I saw her chest was heaving up and down in an angry way.

"No!" I said, and I now felt stronger, as if my true self had finally emerged. So this was what had been inside me all along.

"No! I won't!" I screamed.

She yanked me by the arm, pulled me off the floor, snapped off the TV. She was frighteningly strong, half pulling, half carrying me toward the piano as I kicked the throw rugs under my feet. She lifted me up and onto the hard bench. I was sobbing by now, looking at her bitterly. Her chest was heaving even more and her mouth was open, smiling crazily as if she were pleased I was crying.

"You want me to be someone that I'm not!" I sobbed. "I'll never be the kind of daughter you want me to be!"

"Only two kinds of daughters," she shouted in Chinese. "Those who are obedient and those who follow their own mind! Only one kind of daughter can live in this house. Obedient daughter!"

"Then I wish I wasn't your daughter. I wish you weren't my mother," I shouted. As I said these things I got scared. It felt like worms and toads and slimy things crawling out of my chest, but it also felt good, as if this awful side of me had surfaced, at last.

"Too late change this," said my mother shrilly.

And I could sense her anger rising to its breaking point. I wanted to see it spill over. And that's when I remembered the babies she had lost in China, the ones we never talked about. "Then I wish I'd never been born!" I shouted. "I wish I were dead! Like them."

It was as if I had said the magic words. Alakazam!—and her face went blank, her mouth closed, her arms went slack, and she backed out of the room, stunned, as if she were blowing away like a small brown leaf, thin, brittle, lifeless.

It was not the only disappointment my mother felt in me. In the years that followed, I failed her so many times, each time asserting my own will, my right to fall short of expectations. I didn't get straight As. I didn't become class president. I didn't get into Stanford.[29] I dropped out of college.

For unlike my mother, I did not believe I could be anything I wanted to be. I could only be me.

And for all those years, we never talked about the disaster at the recital[30] or my terrible accusations afterward at the piano bench. All that remained unchecked,[31] like a betrayal that was now unspeakable. So I never found a way to ask her why she had hoped for something so large that failure was inevitable.[32]

And even worse, I never asked her what frightened me the most: Why had she given up hope?

For after our struggle at the piano, she never mentioned my playing again. The lessons stopped. The lid to the piano was closed, shutting out the dust, my misery, and her dreams.

So she surprised me. A few years ago, she offered to give me the piano, for my thirtieth birthday. I had not played in all those years. I saw the offer as a sign of forgiveness, a tremendous burden removed.

"Are you sure?" I asked shyly. "I mean, won't you and Dad miss it?"

"No, this your piano," she said firmly. "Always your piano. You only one can play."

---

[29]Stanford: California university
[30]recital: concert
[31]unchecked: unstoppable
[32]inevitable: sure to happen

"Well, I probably can't play anymore," I said. "It's been years."

"You pick up fast," said my mother, as if she knew this was certain. "You have natural talent. You could been genius if you want to."

"No I couldn't."

"You just not trying," said my mother. And she was neither angry nor sad. She said it as if to announce a fact that could never be disproved. "Take it," she said.

But I didn't at first. It was enough that she had offered it to me. And after that, every time I saw it in my parents' living room, standing in front of the bay windows, it made me feel proud, as if it were a shiny trophy I had won back.

Last week I sent a tuner over to my parents' apartment and had the piano reconditioned, for purely sentimental reasons. My mother had died a few months before and I had been getting things in order for my father, a little bit at a time. I put the jewelry in special silk pouches. The sweaters she had knitted in yellow, pink, bright orange—all the colors I hated—I put those in moth-proof boxes. I found some old Chinese silk dresses, the kind with little slits up the sides. I rubbed the old silk against my skin, then wrapped them in tissue and decided to take them home with me.

After I had the piano tuned, I opened the lid and touched the keys. It sounded even richer than I remembered. Really, it was a very good piano. Inside the bench were the same exercise notes with handwritten scales, the same secondhand music books with their covers held together with yellow tape.

I opened up the Schumann book to the dark little piece I had played at the recital. It was on the left-hand side of the page, "Pleading Child." It looked more difficult than I remembered. I played a few bars, surprised at how easily the notes came back to me.

And for the first time, or so it seemed, I noticed the piece on the right-hand side. It was called "Perfectly Contented." I tried to play this one as well. It had a lighter melody but the same flowing rhythm and turned out to be quite easy. "Pleading Child" was shorter but slower; "Perfectly Contented" was longer, but faster. And after I played them both a few times, I realized they were two halves of the same song.

REFLECT ······································

At the beginning of the story, the daughter says that she was excited about her mother's plans to make her a prodigy. What made her lose her enthusiasm later on?

How do you feel about the daughter's embarrassing experience at the talent show? Are you sorry for her, or do you think she deserved what happened to her? Why do you feel the way you do?

Were you surprised that the mother wanted the daughter to continue taking piano lessons after the talent show? Why did the mother want the daughter to continue?

Reread the last paragraph of the story. What is the meaning of the daughter's discovery? What has the daughter learned about herself?

What does the title "Two Kinds" refer to? Do you think the title has more than one meaning? If so, what are they?

WRITE ·······································

In a turning point in the story, the daughter looks at herself in the mirror and decides to stop trying to do well on her mother's tests. Imagine that you are the daughter, and write a page in your diary explaining the decision.

The daughter says her mother never spoke to her about the talent show. What did the mother think? Imagine that you are she, and write a letter to a close friend describing the show and your daughter's performance.

As an adult, the daughter has a deeper understanding of her mother and their longstanding disagreements and struggles. Describe a serious disagreement that you had with a parent or other adult when you were a child. Then compare and contrast how you felt about the situation as a child with how you feel today. Now that you are older, do you think the adult was right? Explain.

CREDITS